EFFECTIVE
EXECUTIVE'S
GUIDE TO

The Eight Steps for Using Microsoft® Project 2000 to Organize, Manage and Finish Critically Important Projects

PROJECT
2000

D1128816

EFFECTIVE EXECUTIVES GUIDE TO

The Eight Steps for Using Microsoft® Project 2000 to Organize, Manage and Finish Critically Important Projects

PROJECT 2000

Stephen L. Nelson
Pat Coleman
Kaarin Dolliver

REDMOND
TECHNOLOGY
PRESS

Effective Executives Guide to Microsoft® Project 2000:
The Eight Steps for Using Microsoft® Project 2000 to Organize, Manage and Finish Critically Important Projects

Published by
Redmond Technology Press
8581 154th Avenue NE
Redmond, WA 98052
www.redtechpress.com

Library of Congress Catalog Card No: 99-068374

ISBN 0-9672981-1-3

Printed and bound in the United States of America.

9 8 7 6 5 4 3 2 1

Distributed by
Independent Publishers Group
814 N. Franklin St.
Chicago, IL 60610
www.ipgbook.com

Steps at a Glance

Contents

Step 4   **Identify and Allocate Resources**   **57**

Step 5   **Review Project Organization**   **87**

INTRODUCTION

On project managers' office walls, you sometimes see a poster that lists the following five stages in the life cycle of a project:

- Enthusiasm for the goal
- Disillusionment with the progress
- Search for the guilty
- Persecution of the innocent
- Praise for the nonparticipants

As a friend of ours is fond of saying, "It's like a joke, but it's not funny." Unfortunately, we've all managed projects in the past that could be summarized in these words.

If you've picked up this book in the bookstore or if you've just bought this book, you probably have a good reason for doing so. Maybe you've finished managing the project from hell, and you're sure there's a better way. Or maybe you're about to embark on a new project, and your enthusiasm has led you to consider setting it up in Microsoft Project 2000. You might also have used previous versions of Project, and, along with your other preparations for the new millennium, you want your project management tools to be up-to-date.

Whatever the reason, if you're a busy executive, if you manage projects (large and complicated or small and compact), and if plowing through a thousand pages of technical jargon sounds more painful than a root canal, this book is for you. In a nutshell, we walk you through the eight steps of project management using Project 2000. Within each step, we summarize, describe, and list the actions you need to take to set up and record information about your project. We don't tell you everything there is to know about Project because you don't need an encyclopedic knowledge of the program to manage your projects effectively.

Before we get into the details of what you will find in this book, we want to alert you to one of the pitfalls of using project management software. A few years ago, we had a department manager who had become completely enamored with a new project management application. The walls of his office were covered with PERT charts he had printed out and with other charts and diagrams. In essence, this guy spent more time managing his project management program than he did managing his projects. Project 2000 is a tool, not a deliverable. Its purpose is to make your life easier, not to complicate it. And as you'll soon see, this is our approach to using it.

You should also know that we've made some assumptions about you as we wrote this book. First, we assume that you are a knowledgeable and informed executive who has some experience using Microsoft Windows and Windows applications. You know how to use the mouse and how to select menu commands and access tools on a toolbar. Second, you're on speaking terms with the aspects of project management, and third, you're acquainted with the accounting practices that are typically involved in project management. That said, however, we also assume that from time to time you may need some detail, and we've included that where appropriate.

What Is Project 2000?

Microsoft Project 2000 is the latest version of a project management application that has been around since the mid-1980s. You can use it to plan and track the progress of a project using standard approaches to defining projects and organizing the tasks that make up a project, including Gantt charts, PERT charts, and variations on these themes. You can establish a baseline and then track how reality compares with it. You can allocate and monitor people and equipment, and you can track costs and compare them with your budget.

In addition, if you have access to a local area network, an intranet, or the Internet, you can use Project tools to communicate with others, post portions of your project on the Web, and send Project files as e-mail attachments.

When Should You Use Project 2000?

Project 2000 provides most of the tools and techniques you need to manage projects, whether you manage projects with hundreds or thousands of tasks and as many resources or you merely tap into Project's features and functions to think more clearly about organizing simple yet important projects. Regardless of where you fall in this spectrum, you will find that Project delivers five general benefits:

- Using Project lets you answer the question, "What is a project?"

  This might seem obvious, but if you've managed any projects at all, you know that clarifying the use of a resource or assigning a task can become complicated if the project itself is not defined well. Using Project helps you answer this fundamental question.

- Using Project lets you answer the question, "How will the project be accomplished?"

  If you see your project as one gigantic to-do list of random and disconnected tasks, you're going to be overwhelmed and so is anybody involved in the project. Using Project to organize your to-do list into tasks and subtasks and to identify what depends on what lets you see light at the end of the tunnel.

- Using Project lets you answer the question, "When will the project and the parts of the project be completed?"

  Scheduling is essential when managing a project. You need to know when tasks will start and finish so that you can allocate human and equipment resources or perhaps even hire people with special skills. And, unless you have an unlimited amount of time and an unlimited budget (that is, you work in fantasyland), your organization will hold you responsible for the eventual outcome of your project and its completion date. Using Project, you can see at a glance where you are on the schedule and what needs to be done.

- Using Project lets you answer the question, "Who or what will do the work?"

  You may need to answer only the preceding three questions, but if careful management of resources is key to the success of your project, you need Project. With Project's resource management features you can ensure that people and equipment are available on time and within budget.

- Using Project lets you answer the question, "How is my project progressing compared with my plan?"

  When you set up a project in Project, you also establish a baseline plan that you (and Project) use to see how reality is stacking up against the schedule and the costs. Again, unless you work in fantasyland, this is an important issue.

What's in This Book?

As we mentioned earlier, this book is organized according to eight steps of project management. In addition to these steps, we've included four appendixes. Here's a rundown of what you'll find in each step and each appendix.

Step 1: Learn the Language

If you're new to project management, if it's been a long time since you took Project Management 101, or if you need to brush up on some terminology, make reading Step 1 your first step. It's really a project management primer that summarizes the process and then shows you how the process relates to Project 2000.

Step 2: Describe the Project

In this step, you create a project file, save it, resave it, open it again, and set up date parameters and a calendar for your project.

Step 3: Schedule Project Tasks

Here's where you take the to-do list out of your head and commit it to bits and bytes. As you begin to set up an example project, you identify and schedule tasks, specify durations (how long each task will take), insert dependencies (specify which tasks depend on others), add milestones and constraints, and resolve any constraint conflicts.

Step 4: Identify and Allocate Resources

Now it's time to allocate resources (both people and equipment), fine-tune durations, create calendars, review resource allocations, level resources as necessary, assign costs to resources, and share resources if necessary.

Step 5: Review Project Organization

As your plan shapes up, you can use Project to focus on it in various ways to verify that it will work. First, you can display it in outline form, a time-honored technique for imposing organization. You can then change the timescale, and you can filter your project information to display only certain aspects, such as people, tasks, or costs. You can also sort items and display your project in various views.

Step 6: Present Project to Stakeholders

A stakeholder is anyone who is involved in or affected by your project. In this step, you print views of your project, generate and print reports about your project, and take a look at how to send your project file to other applications, including Microsoft Excel, Access, and Word.

Step 7: Manage Project Progress

With your project plan in place, you're ready to start tracking its progress. In this step, you establish a baseline, record completed tasks, update the schedule, set and record costs, compare your progress with your plan, and perform earned value analysis.

Step 8: Communicate Project Status

In this step, you use the tools that Project provides, such as workgroups, to work online—via a local area network, an intranet, or the Internet.

Appendix A: Schedule Project Uncertainties

In Project, you can use the Network Diagram view, also called a PERT chart, to explore various scenarios for your project, including best-case, expected-case, and worst-case. This appendix explains how PERT analysis works and shows you how to access the PERT tools in Project.

Appendix B: Deal with Project Complexity

This appendix explains the tacks you can take when projects become complex. It describes how to simplify dependency relationships, break a large project into smaller projects, use WBS codes to organize projects, and record macros to automate repetitive tasks.

Appendix C: Work with Multiple Projects

If you're like us, you're seldom working with only one project. This appendix shows you how to manage multiple projects with Project.

Appendix D: Customize Project

Project has a slick and easy-to-use interface, but you can change this interface to suit the way you work or prefer to work. This appendix describes how to customize toolbars, menus, column width, and more.

Conventions Used in This Book

To distinguish between Microsoft Project 2000 and your project, we use the word *Project* (with an uppercase P) to refer to Microsoft Project the program. We use the word *project* (with a lowercase p) to refer to your project: the building you're constructing, the information system you're developing, or the marketing campaign you're running.

To identify screen elements, we capitalize the first letter of each word in the description. This convention looks a bit funny at first, but it makes it more likely that you'll understand some instruction such as "click the Cancel—Avoid The Scheduling Conflict button."

You'll also find Notes, Tips, and Warnings, which point out small tidbits of useful information. Pay attention to Warnings; they help you avoid potential problems.

Step 1

LEARN THE LANGUAGE

In This Step

- What is a project?
- What is project management?
- How does Project 2000 help?

I f you're new to project management, the subject might confuse you at first. It encompasses new terms, many behind-the-scenes calculations, and usually the complexities of the project you want to better manage.

To understand project management and effectively manage projects, you need to strip away the clutter, learn the language, and review the logic. This step helps you accomplish the objective of preparing to manage projects by asking and answering three questions:

1. What is a project?

2. What is project management?

3. How does Microsoft Project 2000 help?

When you finish with this step, you should be able to determine whether you really want to use Project 2000 for a particular project and, if so, how you want to use Project 2000.

What Is a Project?

Because people have various conceptions of a "project," it makes sense to start off with a common definition. A project is an activity that has a defined start and a defined finish, produces some measurable result, and requires time, money, and resources to reach completion. Although that definition amounts to a rather abstract description, usually projects are concrete and easy to identify. For example, building a skyscraper, landscaping a parking lot, throwing a party, and making a movie are all projects. Each has a defined start and a defined finish. Each produces some measurable result. Each requires time, money, and resources.

What Is Project Management?

Although the term *management* often refers to loosely defined qualitative activities, the term *project management* actually refers to a rather specific set of four activities related to making sure that you successfully complete a project:

1. Organizing and showing the individual pieces making up a project.

2. Showing the timing of tasks: both the time required to complete tasks and the time tasks start and stop.

3. Identifying and allocating the resources needed to complete a project.

4. Comparing the planned outcome with the actual outcome. Comparisons are usually made in three areas: time spent, resources required, and money spent.

For an example of these four components of project management, suppose that you decide to paint the interior of your apartment. The following section explains how you could set up and manage your project.

NOTE   *The example that follows is intentionally simple. The simplicity makes it easy for you to concentrate on the project management issues involved and not the project.*

Organizing the Pieces Making Up the Project

Even for a small project like painting the interior of your apartment, you benefit by breaking the project into pieces and noting any relationships among them. You might, for example, list six steps for the painting project:

1. Wash the walls you will paint.

2. Plug any holes with patching compound.

3. Tape window and door frames to protect them.

4. Buy the paint and brushes you need.

5. Paint the walls.

6. Clean up after you finish.

Each of these steps is called a *task*. Clearly, you can perform some tasks at the same time. For example, the first four tasks—washing, plugging, taping, and buying—can probably occur in any order. If someone helps, these tasks can even occur at the same time.

However, you need to complete some tasks before you can begin others. For example, you need to complete the first four tasks before you can begin to paint. And you should probably complete the painting before you clean up. These relationships are called *dependencies* because one task depends on another. These relationships are also called *links* because the start of one task is linked to the finish of another task. When one task depends on another, the task that you must finish first is called the *predecessor*. The task that must follow the predecessor is called the *successor*.

Some tasks consist of still smaller tasks or pieces. When a task is made up of multiple parts, these parts are called *subtasks*. For example, you can divide the cleaning-up task into four additional tasks:

1. Locate any paint spills and remove them.

2. Clean the paintbrushes.

3. Remove the tape from around the windows and doorframes.

4. Put away the remaining paint and brushes.

One way you can organize the pieces of a project is by creating a list of tasks and subtasks. You can organize a project in other ways, too.

For example, you can organize project information with a PERT chart, as illustrated in the drawing in Figure 1-1. Figure 1-1 graphically depicts the three main tasks you need to complete for the imaginary painting project.

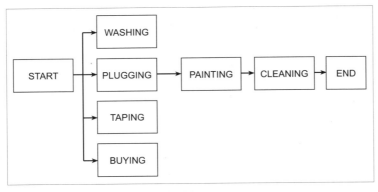

Figure 1-1   An example PERT chart.

PERT is an acronym that stands for Program Evaluation and Review Technique. A PERT chart shows the tasks and the task dependencies of a project. A PERT chart also shows the relationships among tasks. For example, in Figure 1-1, the lines connecting the boxes show the order in which the tasks must be performed.

Listing project tasks and using a PERT chart typically makes a project easier to organize and manage. One big benefit, of course, is that you remember what you need to do to complete the project.

You can also benefit from using a PERT chart because it allows you to visually organize and inspect the relationships among tasks. After reviewing Figure 1-1, for example, you may decide that other dependencies or links exist. Certainly, a PERT chart makes reviewing task dependencies easier.

These two benefits become more important when you manage projects with greater numbers of tasks. Part of the reason is that inadvertently missing a task or dependency is easier when more tasks are involved. Another reason is that when you have large projects, you often tap the skills of more people. If you manage a project with several dozen, several hundred, or several thousand people, achieving project success requires that everyone knows what the project entails and the order in which tasks should be completed.

Showing the Timing of the Tasks

Showing the timing of tasks is the second part of the project-management activity. The timing of tasks consists of two parts: figuring out how much time a task takes and figuring out when a task starts and finishes.

Estimating Task and Project Durations

To show the timing of tasks, you first estimate the amount of time that each task will take. Suppose that you decide to organize the painting project, using the six main tasks. You might make the following estimates:

Washing—3 hours

Plugging—1 hour

Taping—1 hour

Buying—.5 hour

Painting—4 hours

Cleaning—.5 hour

The time taken to complete a task is called its *duration*. For example, the duration of the washing task equals 3 hours, and the duration of the plugging task equals 1 hour.

Some pieces of a project aren't really task1s at all, because their duration equals zero. When the duration of a piece equals zero, the piece is called a *milestone*. Typically, milestones represent events that don't require work—but they are significant points in the project's schedule or life. For example, the Start and End boxes in Figure 1-1 represent milestones.

After you estimate task durations, you can determine how long the project will take to finish by identifying the paths through a project on a PERT chart. To move from the start of the project to the end of the project, you must follow a path. For example, the first path is to start the project with the Washing task, move to the Painting task, and then move to the Cleaning task.

Figure 1-1, in fact, shows four paths, or routes, through the PERT chart:

Path 1: Washing—Painting—Cleaning

Path 2: Plugging—Painting—Cleaning

Path 3: Taping—Painting—Cleaning

Path 4: Buying—Painting—Cleaning

If the term *path* seems confusing, place your finger on the Start box in Figure 1-1 and trace the lines that connect the Start box to the Wash box, the Wash box to the Paint box, the Paint box to the Clean box, and the Clean box to the End box. What you trace with your finger is the first of the four paths.

Each path has a duration that equals the total of the individual task durations making up the path. You can calculate path durations of the four tasks as follows:

Duration of path 1:
Washing:	3.0 hours
Painting:	4.0 hours
Cleaning	0.5 hour
Path:	7.5 hours

Duration of path 2:
Plugging:	1.0 hour
Painting:	4.0 hours
Cleaning	0.5 hour
Path:	5.5 hours

Duration of path 3:
Taping:	1.0 hour
Painting:	4.0 hours
Cleaning	0.5 hour
Path:	5.5 hours

Duration of path 4:
Buying:	0.5 hour
Painting:	4.0 hours
Cleaning	0.5 hour
Path:	5.0 hours

When you know the durations of each of the paths through the project, you know how long the project will take to finish. Assuming you have at least one other person helping you with the first four tasks of the painting project, you can determine a critical path, or an estimate of the project duration (how long the project will take to finish). In the case of the four paths through the painting project, the critical path is the first one, Washing—Painting—Cleaning, which takes 7.5 hours. The project duration, then, equals 7.5 hours. This assumes that other people can do the taping, plugging, and paint purchasing for you.

NOTE *The 7.5-hour duration along the critical path assumes that you paint and clean alone. If someone helps with the painting and cleaning, you can shorten the task durations. Likewise, the project duration can only be as reasonable as the task durations you enter. So the project can also last much longer, especially if you take the unexpected into account. For example, if your dog knocks over a paint can and tracks paint throughout the apartment, the Cleaning task may take several times longer than you expected.*

Project-management systems like Project 2000 calculate the durations of each of the paths through a project, identify the critical path, and give the project duration. In the simple painting project, making the required calculations isn't much work. But when projects include hundreds of tasks and dozens of paths, the time savings are enormous.

At this point, you may be asking yourself why you would want to go to the effort of estimating durations so you can calculate the critical path. You will usually want to know your project's critical path for three reasons.

First, because the duration of the critical path equals the duration of the project, identifying the critical path lets you estimate when you will finish the project. In the case of the painting project, because the critical path equals 7.5 hours, you know that once you start the project, it will take at least 7.5 hours to complete.

Second, if you know which tasks are on the critical path, you know which tasks cannot be delayed without delaying the project. For example, the Painting task is on the critical path. If painting takes longer than 4 hours, your project takes longer than 7.5 hours.

Third, if you know which tasks aren't on the critical path, you know which tasks can be delayed without delaying the project. For example, the Buying task isn't on the critical path. So, to some extent, the Buying task can be delayed without delaying the project. The amount of time a task can be delayed without delaying the project is called *slack*. To determine the actual amount of slack, you need to know when a task can start and when a task must finish, which is the subject of the next section.

Using Start and Finish Dates and Times

Start and finish dates and times make up a second aspect of the timing of tasks. You must calculate four dates and times for each task: early start, early finish, late start, and late finish. The early start shows the earliest date or time you can begin work on a task. The early finish shows the earliest date or time you can expect to complete a task. The late start shows the latest date or time you can begin work on a task without delaying the project. The late finish shows the latest date or time you can complete a task without delaying the project.

Does any of this information—knowing when tasks need to be initiated and completed—help? Yes, especially if you have a large number of tasks in a project, because tracking a large number of tasks is more difficult.

The arithmetic for calculating start and finish dates and times isn't difficult, but it is rather tedious. Thankfully, Project 2000 performs the arithmetic for you. However, because you use the start and finish dates in your decision-making, you may benefit from understanding the calculations.

NOTE   *If you don't want this knowledge, skip the following set of action descriptions.*

To calculate the start and finish dates for tasks and for the project, perform the following actions:

1. **Identify when you will start the project.**

   Suppose that in the painting example, you decide you will start next Monday at 8 A.M. The project start time, then, equals 8 A.M.

2. **Calculate the finish time of the project.**

   You do this by adding the durations of all the tasks in the critical path to the project start. For example, in the case of the painting project, you start with the project start time of 8 A.M. and then add the 3 hours of washing, the 4 hours of painting, and the 0.5 hour of cleaning. This formula gives you the finish time, 3:30 P.M.

3. **Calculate the early start of each task.**

   Starting with the first task in each path, calculate the early start of each task in the path by adding the duration of the predecessor task to the early start time of the predecessor task. For the first task in a path, because there is no predecessor task, use the project start.

This sounds confusing, but it isn't. For example, make the following calculations to determine the early starts for the tasks in the first path, washing—painting—cleaning:

Early start of Washing task:

8 A.M. (project start)

+ 0 hours (no predecessor task)

= 8 A.M. (early start of Washing task)

Early start of Painting task:

8 A.M. (project start)

+ 3 hours (duration of Washing task)

= 11 A.M. (early start of Painting task)

Early start of Cleaning task:

11 A.M. (project start)

+ 4 hours (duration of Painting task)

= 3 P.M. (early start of Cleaning task)

In a similar fashion, you can also calculate the early starts of each task in the remaining paths. The only twist is when a task appears on more than one path. For example, the two tasks of Painting and Cleaning appear on all four paths of the painting project:

Path 1: Washing—Painting—Cleaning

Path 2: Plugging—Painting—Cleaning

Path 3: Taping—Painting—Cleaning

Path 4: Buying—Painting—Cleaning

So you end up calculating an early start for the Painting and Cleaning tasks for each of the four paths through the project. The obvious question is, which of the four early starts is correct? The answer is that when you calculate more than one early start, the latest early start is the correct one.

This sounds tricky, but it really isn't. Take the case of the first four tasks in the painting project. If you make the calculations of the Painting task's early start for each of the four paths, you get these four early starts:

Path 1: 8 A.M. + 3 hours washing = 11 A.M. early start

Path 2: 8 A.M. + 1 hour plugging = 9 A.M. early start

Path 3: 8 A.M. + 1 hour taping = 9 A.M. early start

Path 4: 8 A.M. + 0.5 hour buying = 8:30 A.M. early start

4. Calculate the early finish of each task.

Once you calculate the early start of each task, you can calculate the early finish of each task by adding the duration of the task to the early start of the task. For example, to calculate the early finish of the Washing task, add the early start of the washing task (8 A.M.) to the duration of the Washing task (3 hours). The early finish of the Washing task equals 11 A.M.

In this example, the latest of the early starts is 11 A.M., which is when the Washing task finishes. Because you cannot start painting until you finish washing, picking the latest of the early start dates means you're sure that you have completed the predecessor tasks that finish last.

Table 1-1 shows the early start and finish times you would calculate for the painting project as part of actions 3 and 4.

TASK NAME	TASK DURATION	EARLY START	EARLY FINISH
Washing	3.00	8:00 A.M.	11:00 A.M.
Plugging	1.00	8:00 A.M.	9:00 A.M.
Taping	1.00	8:00 A.M.	9:00 A.M.
Buying	0.50	8:00 A.M.	8:30 A.M.
Painting	4.00	11:00 A.M.	3:00 P.M.
Cleaning	0.50	3:00 P.M.	3:30 P.M.

Table 1-1   The early start and finish times.

5. Calculate the late finish of each of the paths.

Starting with the last task in each of the paths, calculate the late finish of each task in each path by subtracting the duration of the successor task from the late finish of the successor task. For the last task in a path, because there is no successor path, use the project finish. For example, make the following calculations to determine the late finishes for the tasks in the first path, Washing—Painting—Cleaning:

Late finish of Cleaning task:

3:30 P.M. (project finish)

- 0 hours (no successor task)

= 3:30 P.M. (late finish of Washing task)

Late finish of Painting task:

3:30 P.M. (late finish of Cleaning task)

- 0.5 hour (duration of Cleaning task)

= 3 P.M. (late finish of Painting task)

Late finish of Washing task:

3 P.M. (late finish of Painting task)

- 4 hours (duration of Painting task)

= 11 A.M. (late finish of Washing task)

In a similar fashion, you also calculate the late finishes of tasks in each of the remaining paths. But as with calculating the early starts, however, there is a twist: When a task appears on more than one path, you end up calculating several late finishes. For example, the two tasks of Painting and Cleaning appear in all four paths for the painting project:

Path 1: Washing—Painting—Cleaning

Path 2: Plugging—Painting—Cleaning

Path 3: Taping—Painting—Cleaning

Path 4: Buying—Painting—Cleaning

So you must calculate four late finish times for the Painting and Cleaning tasks for each of the four paths through the project. In this example, you end up calculating the same late finish times because the two tasks that lay on all four paths are the last two tasks on each. Often, however, you will calculate different latest finishes. And when you do, use the earliest late finish.

6. **Calculate the late start of each task.**

Once you calculate the late finish of each task, you can calculate the late start of each task by subtracting the duration of the task from its late finish. For example, to calculate the late start of the Buying task, subtract the Buying task duration, 0.5 hour, from the late finish of the Buying task, which Table 1-2 shows as 11 A.M. Table 1-2 also shows the latest start and finish times that you would calculate for the painting project as part of actions 5 and 6.

TASK NAME	TASK DURATION	LATE START	LATE FINISH
Washing	3.00	8:00 A.M.	11:00 A.M.
Plugging	1.00	10:00 A.M.	11:00 A.M.
Taping	1.00	10:00 A.M.	11:00 A.M.
Buying	0.50	10:30 A.M.	11:00 A.M.
Painting	4.00	11:00 A.M.	3:00 P.M.
Cleaning	0.50	3:00 P.M.	3:30 P.M.

Table 1-2   The latest start and finish times.

7. Calculate task slack.

After you've calculated the early and late start and finish times, you can calculate the slack. To do this, calculate the difference between the early and late start or the difference between the early and late finish. Either calculation produces the same result because the task duration determines the difference between the early start and finish and between the late start and finish. Table 1-3 shows these differences calculated both ways. The difference equals the amount of slack in a task—the amount that a task start or finish can be delayed without delaying the project. Tasks on the critical path show zero slack, which means that any delay in completing those tasks delays the project. However, it is helpful to know, for example, that you can delay the Buying task start as much as 2.5 hours without delaying the project.

TASK NAME	TASK DURATION	EARLY START	EARLY FINISH	LATE START	LATE FINISH	SLACK TIME
Washing	3.00	8:00 A.M.	11:00 A.M.	8:00 A.M.	11:00 A.M.	0.00
Plugging	1.00	8:00 A.M.	9:00 A.M.	10:00 A.M.	11:00 A.M.	2.00
Taping	1.00	8:00 A.M.	9:00 A.M.	10:00 A.M.	11:00 A.M.	2.00
Buying	0.50	8:00 A.M.	8:30 A.M.	10:30 A.M.	11:00 A.M.	2.50
Painting	4.00	11:00 A.M.	3:00 P.M.	11:00 A.M.	3:00 P.M.	0.00
Cleaning	0.50	3:00 P.M.	3:30 P.M.	3:00 P.M.	3:30 P.M.	0.00

Table 1-3   Calculating slack.

Identifying and Allocating Project Resources

The third aspect of project management is identifying and allocating the resources you require to complete a project. Typically, you need both people and equipment to complete tasks. And because resources are limited, you usually need to organize your projects with an eye to available resources.

Take, again, the example project of painting your apartment. If you add the durations of all the tasks, the project in total requires 10 hours of time from one or more persons. That's a resource. If you're painting the ceilings, the project probably requires ladders or step stools. Those are resources, too.

Because projects usually require resources—both people and equipment—you want to make sure that your plans assume realistic use of any resources.

Here are the general actions you take to recognize the resources planned for a project:

1. List the resources you have available.

2. Allocate resources to project tasks.

3. Adjust for any discrepancies between the resources you have available and the resources you need.

In listing the available resources, include both people and equipment. For the painting project, for example, your people resources probably include yourself and perhaps a helpful friend. Your equipment resources may include a ladder, paintbrushes, a paint roller and pan, and drop cloths to protect your furniture and carpet from paint. You can actually create a resources list from this information:

Me

My best friend

A 10-foot ladder

Two paintbrushes

A paint roller and pan

Two 10-by-16-foot drop cloths

In allocating resources, you commit a resource to a task and, as a result, take it off the list of available resources for the time that you've scheduled it. If you allocate your best friend to the task of washing the walls, for example, remove him or her from the resources list. If you allocate the use of the ladder for plugging holes with patching compound, remove the ladder from the resources list.

After you complete the first two steps of recognizing project resources, you need to resolve any discrepancies between what the project needs and what you actually have available to allocate. Essentially, you want to verify that neither of the following two error conditions exists:

1. Resource shortages

2. Resource overallocations

Resource shortages refer to situations in which you need a resource for a task, but the resource is not available. If your painting project calls for you, a single individual, to complete the painting within the 7.5-hour project duration, you need more than one person because the project amounts to 10 hours of work.

Resource overallocations refer to situations in which you allocate a resource to different tasks that use the same resource at the same time. If your painting project calls for the ladder to be used simultaneously—by you as you plug holes and by your best friend when he or she washes the walls—a resource overallocation exists.

NOTE   *A resource overallocation also occurs when a task requires more time than a resource can provide. For example, if a person works 8 hours a day but a task requires 16 hours a day of work, the person is overallocated.*

The process of rescheduling a project's tasks so that resource overallocations are eliminated is called *resource leveling*. Resource leveling generally involves stretching out the work on tasks so that resources are used more evenly. If necessary, however, resource leveling can also stretch out the critical path.

In the painting project, for example, the project's critical path is 7.5 hours and the project requires 10 hours of work. If you can't get a friend's help and therefore end up doing all 10 hours of work yourself, you won't be able to finish the 10-hour project in a mere 7.5 hours. You'll be overallocated. Your only recourse—assuming you can't recruit another friend/resource—would be to stretch out the 10 hours of work over 10 or more hours. In this case, you would be leveling resources.

With only a handful of tasks and a short list of resources, identifying and allocating resources might not be worth the effort. Most projects, however, do benefit from resource allocation and leveling. Even in relatively small projects, forgetting about a resource or inadvertently overallocating a resource is all too easy.

Monitoring Project Time, Resources, and Costs

The fourth component of project management consists of monitoring the actual time spent on tasks, the actual resources used by tasks, and the actual cost of a project. Traditionally, you monitor these three characteristics—time, resources, and cost—by comparing what you planned with what actually occurs.

Sometimes this business of comparing planned figures with actual figures gives you unfavorable results. Unfortunately, the comparisons often show that a project is progressing more slowly, is using more resources, and is costing more money than you originally planned. However, the comparisons provide you with an early warning system. And, often, the early warnings give you time to remedy problems when they are little rather than big.

A common technique used in monitoring project time, resources, and costs is earned value analysis. Earned value analysis refers to the very logical process of comparing the planned progress and cost of some task with the actual progress and cost.

Take the Painting task in the example apartment-painting project. If the project schedule indicates that this task will take 4 hours, starting at 11 A.M. and finishing at 3 P.M., you can use this information to manage the completion of the task. To do so, simply compare the planned work with the actual work to see whether work is progressing at the planned rate. For example, you could verify that painting begins at 11 A.M. and verify at periodic intervals that work continues at the planned rate. For example, you could verify at 12 P.M., 1 hour into the planned painting task, that someone has actually been painting for an hour. You could verify at 1 P.M., 2 hours into the painting project, that someone has actually been painting for 2 hours, and so on.

NOTE   *Comparing planned work with actual work might be done on the basis of hours as illustrated in the preceding paragraph. Such comparisons can also be performed using cost. In the case of the painting project, if you were paying your friend $10 an hour, you could also check to see that you had incurred $10 of painting cost after 1 hour, $20 after 2 hours, and so on.*

The comparison of planned work with actual work is often very useful for assessing whether resources are working according to your schedule or plan, but unfortunately, the comparison doesn't indicate whether your original duration estimates are reasonable.

You can often make another comparison that lets you assess the goodness of your duration estimates, however. You can compare the planned work scheduled in some interval to planned work performed in some interval.

Suppose, for the sake of simplicity, that in the imaginary painting project, you will paint four walls but not the ceiling. Further suppose that all four walls are roughly the same amount of work. In this case, you could also say, because the task duration is estimated as 4 hours, that your plan is to paint one wall each hour. At 12 P.M., 1 hour into the Painting task, you could verify not only that someone has been painting for an hour but that he or she has painted one of the four walls. If the person has been painting an hour but hasn't yet finished a wall, you would know that your original duration estimates were suspect.

NOTE *The key to making comparisons of actual work performed and planned work performed is to have some metric that quantifies the actual work.*

Figure 1-2 shows an earned value graph that plots planned work scheduled, actual work performed, and planned work performed. What the graph shows in this case is that the original task duration of the Painting task was low but that by applying extra resources the project still finished by 3 P.M.

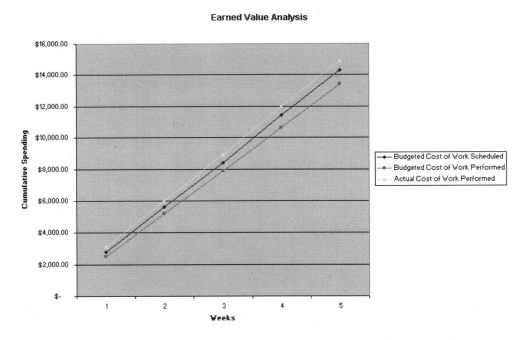

Figure 1-2   An earned value graph compares planned work scheduled, actual work performed, and planned work performed.

How Does Project 2000 Help?

Project 2000 includes features that help you with each of the four components of project management you just examined: organizing and showing the individual pieces making up a project; showing the timing of tasks; identifying and allocating the resources needed to complete a project; and comparing the planned outcome with the actual outcome by making comparisons in the areas of time spent, resources required, and money spent.

Essentially, Project provides you with a collection of tools for creating project schedules, and then provides you with still other tools and numerous reports that you can use to view project information in different ways, analyze the project and track its progress, and communicate about the project with other people.

NOTE *Many tools, views, and reports perform two and sometimes even three of the four components of project management.*

Using Project to Organize and Show the Pieces of a Project

Project provides one view of a project that is particularly powerful for listing project tasks and visualizing and linking the tasks that make up the project: Gantt Chart view. Most of the time you work with Project, you'll probably use this view.

The Gantt Chart view includes two sections, as shown in Figure 1-3. The Gantt table on the left lists the pieces of the project and contains information about them. The Gantt chart on the right shows the tasks of the project as horizontal bars plotted against a time-scale, so you can see how long tasks take, when tasks start, and when tasks finish. Figure 1-3 shows a Gantt chart of the painting project.

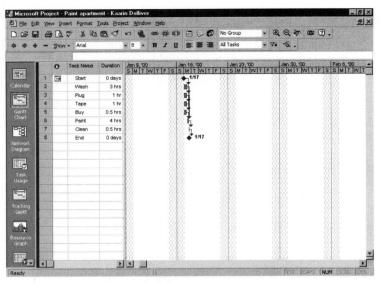

Figure 1-3   A Gantt chart.

Project also allows you to create PERT charts, which it calls Network Diagrams, as described earlier in the chapter and illustrated in Figure 1-1. Network Diagrams provide an excellent format for visually showing the tasks of a project and the order in which the tasks must be completed. Figure 1-4 shows a Network Diagram in Project.

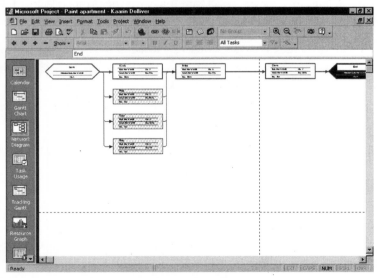

Figure 1-4   A Network Diagram in Project.

When Project draws a Network Diagram, it includes several details about each task in the task's box. The box names the task, lists the duration and ID number, specifies the date the task begins and ends, and lists the progress on the task and the resource assigned to the task. Project's Network Diagrams display milestones as rectangles, critical tasks as hexagons, and summary tasks as octagons. The Project interface looks a little different from the standard in Figure 1-4, and the boxes look small because to show the entire project at once, we needed to maximize the viewable area and zoom out on the chart.

Using Project to Show the Timing of Tasks

The Gantt Chart view, as described above, shows the timing of tasks, but to better see the to-do list for a certain period of time, you can use Project's Calendar view as shown in Figure 1-5.

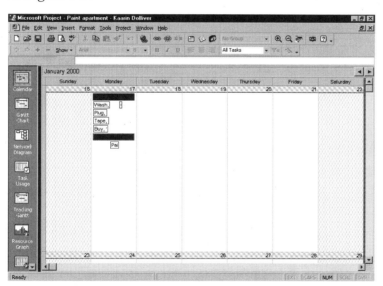

Figure 1-5　The Calendar view.

If you double-click the date header with the painting project, Project displays the list of tasks scheduled for that day, as shown in Figure 1-6.

	Name	Duration	Start	Finish
✓	Start	0d	Mon 1/17/00	Mon 1/17/00
✓	Wash	3h	Mon 1/17/00	Mon 1/17/00
✓	Clean	0.5h	Mon 1/17/00	Mon 1/17/00
✓	Plug	1h	Mon 1/17/00	Mon 1/17/00
✓	Tape	1h	Mon 1/17/00	Mon 1/17/00
✓	Buy	0.5h	Mon 1/17/00	Mon 1/17/00
✓	End	0d	Mon 1/17/00	Mon 1/17/00
✓	Paint	4h	Mon 1/17/00	Mon 1/17/00

Figure 1-6   A to-do list for a day.

NOTE   *To change the time span shown in the Calendar view, choose the View menu's Zoom command and select a different time span in the Zoom dialog box.*

Using Project to Manage Resources

Project also provides tools and reports that allow you to manage project resources. To verify that you have remembered to allocate resources to each of the tasks making up a project, you can view the Gantt chart. The rightmost column of information in the table shows the assigned resource. The bars in the chart also name the resource (see Figure 1-7). And, obviously, any tasks that don't show resources may need resources assigned.

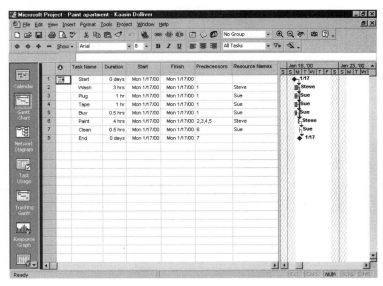

Figure 1-7   A Gantt chart with an expanded task area so you can see assigned resources.

To verify that you haven't overallocated a resource, you can view a Resource Graph like the one shown in Figure 1-8. By comparing allocated resources with the actual resources available, you can ascertain whether you're planning to use more of a resource—a person or some piece of equipment—than is available.

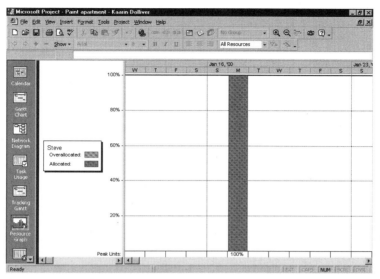

Figure 1-8   A resource graph.

NOTE   *It's impossible to see in a black-and-white image like that shown in Figure 1-8, but resource graphs identify overallocations using red bars.*

Another useful tool for more closely exploring why resource allocations exist is the Resource Sheet, as shown in Figure 1-9. A Resource Sheet lists resource allocations by task and then totals individual task-level resource allocations in order to calculate a total allocation.

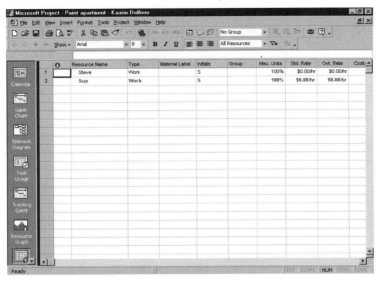

Figure 1-9　A Resource Sheet.

In a simple project like the apartment painting example used throughout this chapter, such a Resource Sheet may not seem useful. In larger projects—those with dozens of tasks and resources—such a Resource Sheet lets you more easily see who is being overscheduled and who is being underscheduled.

One other noteworthy resource management feature of Project concerns its resource leveling tools. Project will level resources. In other words, you can direct Project to stretch out the work on tasks where slack is available. When Project levels resources, it smoothes out and reschedules resource usage to avoid or at least minimize overallocation.

NOTE　*Resource leveling is described in "Step 4: Identify and Allocate Resources."*

Using Project to Monitor Projects

The fourth and final component of project management is monitoring project time, resources, and cost by comparing planned work scheduled with actual work performed and with planned work performed. Project allows you to collect a complete set of planned and actual project time, resources, and cost information. You should be able to monitor carefully any of the three factors. Figure 1-10, for example, shows the Tracking Gantt view, which lets you easily compare actual time and progress with your original estimate, or baseline.

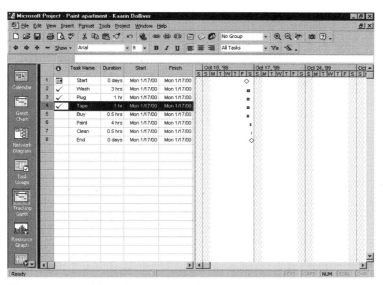

Figure 1-10　A Tracking Gantt chart.

NOTE　*Establishing a baseline and comparing it with actual progress is described in "Step 7: Manage Project Progress."*

Summary

This first step gets you started by explaining the language and logic of project management. To accomplish this, the step describes what a project is and identifies the four components of project management: organizing the pieces that make up a project; showing the timing of project tasks; identifying and allocating project resources; and monitoring project time, resources, and cost. This step also describes in general terms how you can use Project to help with each of these four tasks.

In "Step 2: Describe the Project," you begin reading about the process of describing a project to Project so you can use its tools to plan, organize, and monitor a project.

Step 2

DESCRIBE THE PROJECT

Tasks Required to Complete the Step

- Creating a project file
- Setting project start and finish dates
- Setting up a project calendar

In order to use Microsoft Project 2000, you must begin by describing the project in very general terms. This first step includes creating the Project file you will use for storing all the project information.

Creating a Project File

Predictably, you store project information in a file. You can postpone the actual creation until you record the last bit of project information, but it makes most sense to create the file first. This way, you can easily save your changes as you work (and also have Project periodically save your changes automatically).

Saving a Project File for the First Time

To create an empty project file, take the following actions:

1. Start Project.

You start Project in the same way that you start other Microsoft Windows programs. For example, click the Start button, choose Programs, and then click Microsoft Project. Project starts and opens a new, blank project file. Figure 2-1 shows the Microsoft Project window with an empty project file.

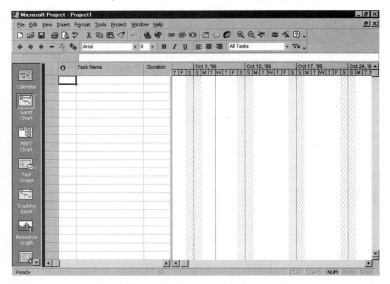

Figure 2-1   The Microsoft Project window with an empty project file.

NOTE   *You may have Project set up to display the Project Help file when you start the program. To close Help, click the Help window's Close box. To tell Project that you don't want it to display the Help file when you start the program, clear the Display Help At Startup check box in the Help window.*

NOTE   *After you create a project file, you can also start Project by telling Windows to open the project file by choosing the project file from the Documents menu or by using Windows Explorer to open the document.*

2. Save the new project.

You can save a new project in two ways. You can choose the File menu's Save As command. Or, if a project file hasn't yet been saved, you can click the Save toolbar button. Project displays the Save As dialog box, as shown in Figure 2-2.

Figure 2-2   The Save As dialog box.

3. Choose a folder location for the new project file.

To save the file in a common location for documents, click one of the icons on the left side of the Save As dialog box:

- If you have Windows 95 or 98, click the My Documents icon to save the file to the default storage location for Office documents.

- If you have Windows NT, click the Personal icon.

- To save the file to the Windows desktop, click the Desktop icon.

NOTE   *For more information about Web Folders and sharing Project files with others over the Internet or an intranet, see Appendix C.*

To save the file to a location other than one designated by an icon (such as a network drive), use the Save In drop-down list box and the large list box below to select the drive and folder location.

TIP   *Use the Up One Level toolbar button to move up from a subfolder to its parent folder.*

4. Name the project file.

Enter a name for the file in the File Name text box. You don't need to add a file extension—Project automatically does this for you. Project allows you to enter very long filenames if you want, but if you do use long names, make sure that the first few characters clearly identify the workbook so it is easy to find later on.

5. Select a file format from the Save As Type drop-down list box.

If you're the only one who will be using the file, you can accept the default, Project. If you'll be sharing the file with other people who will use a different version of Project, select the format they'll be using or select a format that both you and the other user can read. For example, if you use Project 2000 but other people use Project 98, select the Project 98 file format.

NOTE   *Selecting such a file type other than Project (which is the Project 2000 format) may result in the loss of functionality.*

NOTE   *If you imagine basing future Project files on the one you're currently creating, you can save the file as a template. If your projects are often similar, templates are useful tools. In the template file, you can save common items such as formatting and tasks commonly performed in your projects.*

6. Optionally, protect access to the file.

Click the Tools button in the Save As dialog box and then choose the General Options command. Project displays the Save Options dialog box, as shown in Figure 2-3. To prevent unauthorized access to the file, enter a password in the Protection Password box. To protect unauthorized modification of the file, enter a password in the Write Reservation Password box. If you want Project to prompt users to open the file as read-only, select the Read-Only Recommended check box.

Figure 2-3   The Save Options dialog box.

7. Click Save.

Project saves the file in the specified location and format using whatever name you choose.

Resaving a Project File

After you save a project file for the first time, you can click the Save toolbar button or choose the File menu's Save command to resave the file. You need to resave the file to save any changes you make to the project file.

After you've added tasks to a project (Step 3 describes how to do this) and you attempt to save it, Project displays a message box, as shown in Figure 2-4, asking whether you want to save the project with or without a baseline.

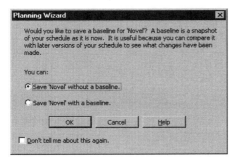

Figure 2-4   Saving a project with a baseline.

A baseline is essentially a snapshot of your project, against which you can track actual progress. You probably want to postpone creating a baseline until the planning phase of the project is mostly complete and you have reasonable confidence in the schedule. Step 7 describes in detail how to create and edit baselines.

If you want to create a new project file using the open project file, you can choose the File menu's Save As command and specify a new filename and location.

Opening Project Files

Opening project files is closely related to saving project files. To later open a project file, take the following actions:

1. Click the Open toolbar button.

Project displays the Open dialog box, as shown in Figure 2-5.

TIP   *To open a Project file you've recently saved, you don't need to display the Open dialog box. Simply choose the file's name from the bottom of the File menu.*

Figure 2-5 The Open dialog box.

2. Open the folder storing the file.

Use the icons along the left side, the Look In drop-down list box, and the large list box of folders and files to locate the file. When you find it, select it by clicking it.

- To open a file you've recently accessed, click the History icon to browse short-cuts to recently accessed files.

- If you have Windows 95 or 98, click the My Documents icon to open a file in the default storage location for Office documents.

- If you have Windows NT, click the Personal icon.

- To open a file on the Windows desktop, click the Desktop icon.

To open the file in a location other than one designated by an icon (such as a network drive), use the Look In drop-down list box and the large list box below to select the drive and folder location.

3. Open the file.

When you find the project file you want to open, double-click it to open it.

TIP   *Project allows you to open multiple project files, displaying each in its own document window. To move to another document window, choose the project file from the Window menu.*

Using File Properties

Optionally, you can use the File menu's Properties command to collect or store additional miscellaneous information about the newly created project file.

To use the File menu's Properties command in this manner, choose the command and click the Summary tab. Project displays the Properties dialog box, as shown in Figure 2-6. You can use the boxes provided to record such items as the author, company, and any comments.

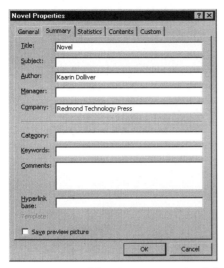

Figure 2-6   The Summary tab of the Properties dialog box.

Setting Project Start and Finish Dates

After you've created the new project file, you next need to identify either the project start or finish date as the date you'll use to anchor the project schedule.

It typically makes sense to anchor the project using a start date and then work from there. In this way, you implicitly base your schedule on when you can start and the descriptions of the tasks that make up your schedule.

If you want to anchor the project using a finish date—which is often risky because this decision tends to be made without regard to the actual project effort—you can do so. With this approach, you implicitly say that completing the project on time is more important than other project characteristics—such as the project costs and the quality of the deliverable.

WARNING   *In general, you shouldn't anchor a project to a finish date unless you're experienced in organizing and managing projects like the one you're describing.*

To identify the project start and finish dates, take the following actions:

1. Choose the Project menu's Project Information command.

Project displays the Project Information dialog box, as shown in Figure 2-7.

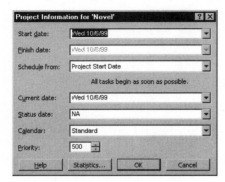

Figure 2-7   The Project Information dialog box.

2. Set the start date.

Click the Start Date box. Then enter the start date.

3. Set the finish date.

Click the Finish Date box. Then enter the finish date.

NOTE   *Click the down arrow at the end of the Start Date box or Finish Date box to display a pop-up monthly calendar you can use to select a date. To select a date shown on the calendar, click the day. To move to another month, click the Back and Forward buttons.*

4. Click OK.

Project saves the start and finish date information and closes the Project Information dialog box.

Setting Up a Project Calendar

Project supplies a standard calendar, which identifies days and dates and some common nonworking days. But to complete your description of the project, you'll want to fine-tune this calendar so it reflects any local customs or company conventions about, for example, holidays.

To set up a project calendar that accurately describes the working dates available within the project start and finish dates, take the following actions:

1. Choose the Tools menu's Change Working Time command.

Project displays the Change Working Time dialog box, as shown in Figure 2-8.

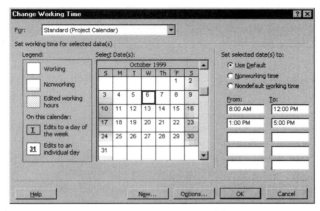

Figure 2-8   The Change Working Time dialog box.

2. Indicate you want to create a new calendar.

Click the New button to tell Project you want to create a new calendar of working and nonworking time. Project displays the Create New Base Calendar dialog box, as shown in Figure 2-9.

Figure 2-9   The Create New Base Calendar dialog box.

3. Name the new base calendar.

Enter the name you want to use for the project calendar.

If the calendar's schedule of working and nonworking days will be specifically for the project, you might want to name it in a way that clearly identifies the connection to the project. A calendar for a plant relocation project might be named Plant Relocation Calendar.

If the calendar's schedule of working and nonworking days will work for other projects you or your company manages, you might want to name it in a way that clearly makes this distinction. A calendar for Acme Distributing might be named Standard Acme Calendar.

4. Copy an existing schedule's information as a starting point.

Click the Make A Copy Of option button, select one of the existing calendars of working and nonworking time from the drop-down list box, and then click OK. Table 2-1 describes each of the three standard calendars you can copy to create a starting point for your own calendar.

CALENDAR	DEFAULT WORKING TIMES
Standard	8 A.M. to 5 P.M., five days a week
Night Shift	11 P.M. to 8 A.M., five days a week
24 Hours	12 A.M. to 12 A.M., seven days a week

Table 2-1   Descriptions of default project calendars you can copy.

5. Describe the typical workweek and workday.

When Project redisplays the Change Working Time dialog box after you click OK at the end of the last action, click the Options button. When Project displays the Calendar tab of the Options dialog box, as shown in Figure 2-10, describe the typical workweek and workday:

- Use the Week Starts On and Fiscal Year Starts In boxes to indicate when the workweek and work year begin.

- Use the Default Start Time and Default End Time boxes to indicate when the workday typically starts and ends.

- Use the Hours Per Day, Hours Per Week, and Days Per Month boxes to indicate how many hours are available in a day and week and how many days are available in a typical month.

Click OK when you finish making these specifications to return to the Change Working Time dialog box.

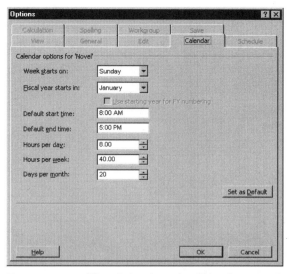

Figure 2-10 The Calendar tab of the Options dialog box.

NOTE *Project uses the Hours Per Day, Hours Per Week, and Days Per Month values to convert the task durations you enter from one time measurement to another time measurement. If you indicate a task will take one month, for example, Project assumes that's the same thing as twenty days if the Days Per Month value is set to 20. If you indicate a task will take one day, Project assumes that's the same thing as eight hours if the Hours Per Day value is set to 8.*

6. Identify project nonworking days.

To identify nonworking days, such as company holidays, use the calendar shown on the Change Working Time dialog box to show the month with the holidays. You can move backward or forward in the calendar by dragging the slider on the vertical scroll bar next to the calendar.

When the month you want shows, press and hold down the Ctrl key and click each of the days you want to mark as nonworking days.

After you've done this, click the Nonworking Time option button. Figure 2-11 shows November 23, 2000, and November 24, 2000, marked as nonworking days.

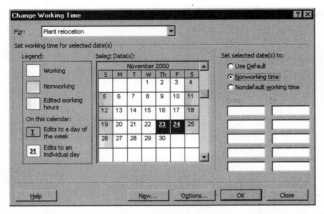

Figure 2-11 The Change Working Time dialog box showing nonworking days.

TIP   *Different countries and localities often use different work calendars. If you're managing a project that includes people in Canada and Japan, for example, you won't be able to create a standard calendar that works for people in both locations. In this case, what you need to do is create a very general project calendar that doesn't identify unique cultural or country holidays. Instead, what you'll need to do is deal with these calendar issues at the resource calendar level. Resource calendars are described in "Step 4: Identify and Allocate Resources."*

7. Describe exceptions to the typical workday or workweek.

To identify any exceptions to the typical workday or workweek, use the calendar shown on the Change Working Time dialog box to show the month with the exceptions.

When the month you want shows, press and hold down the Ctrl key and click each of the days with the exception.

After you do this, click the Nondefault Working Time option button and use the From and To boxes to describe the exception. Figure 2-12 shows January 10, 2001, as just a four-hour workday, which is an exception to the typical eight-hour workday.

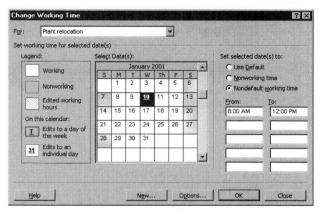

Figure 2-12 The Change Working Time dialog box—this time showing an exception to the usual eight-hour workday.

NOTE *The Change Working Time dialog box provides a legend explaining how working, nonworking, and nondefault working times appear on the calendar.*

8. Save your calendar changes.

Click OK to save your calendar changes. To save the project file with all your changes, click the Save toolbar button.

NOTE *When you're finished working in Project and have saved your changes, click the Close button in the upper right corner of the Microsoft Project window to close Project. If you've made changes to open projects and haven't saved these changes, Project prompts you to do so.*

If you want to make the calendar available for use in other projects, you need to also add the calendar to the global template. For example, if you followed the procedures above to create a company calendar, you would probably want to use this calendar in future projects. To add a calendar to the global Project template, take the following actions:

1. Choose the Tools menu's Organizer command.

Project displays the Organizer dialog box.

2. Click the Calendars tab.

Figure 2-13 shows this tab. By default, the calendars available in the open Project file appear on the right and the calendars available in the global template appear on the left. The drop-down list boxes at the bottom of the dialog box specify which project or template is displayed.

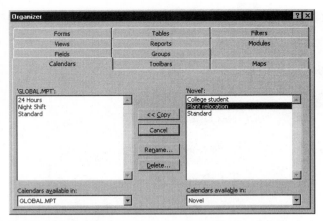

Figure 2-13   The Calendars tab of the Organizer dialog box.

3. Select the calendar you want to copy to the global template, and click the Copy button.

Project adds the calendar to the list on the left.

4. When you're finished, click the dialog box's Close button.

Click the small button with an x in the upper right corner of the dialog box to close the dialog box.

TIP   *To remove a calendar you've erroneously added or no longer need, display the Organizer dialog box, select the calendar you want to remove, and click the Remove button. Note that if you included the calendar in multiple templates, you'll need to remove it from each template.*

Summary

The first step you take to use Project 2000—the step of describing your project in general terms—isn't difficult. All you're doing, essentially, is describing the window of time into which your project needs to fit. But this important step lays a foundation for the next two steps you take, "Step 3: Schedule Project Tasks" and "Step 4: Identify and Allocate Resources."

Step 3

SCHEDULE PROJECT TASKS

Tasks Required to Complete the Step

- Creating a to-do list of tasks and durations
- Collecting additional task information
- Fine-tuning duration values
- Identifying task dependencies
- Adding other scheduling goals and constraints

After you complete "Step 2: Describe the Project," you can accurately describe and schedule the project's tasks. Fortunately, this step isn't much more difficult than creating a well-thought-out to-do list.

Creating a To-Do List of Tasks and Durations

While it's easy to let the work and complexity of a project overwhelm project team participants, you'll often find it quite straightforward to think about a project as a thorough to-do list.

Describing an Example Project

For example, consider the project of publishing a document such as a book or report. At the highest level, you might say such a project consists of three tasks:

1. Write the book.

2. Print the book.

3. Sell the book.

If these tasks were really groups of tasks requiring work from one or more than one person—as is typical—you might further expand this to-do list to a series of tasks and subtasks:

1. Write the book.

   A. Research the book's content.

   B. Create an outline.

   C. Write the rough draft.

   D. Edit the rough draft to create a final manuscript.

2. Print the book.

   A. Prepare the book for printing by desktop publishing.

   B. Print the book.

3. Sell the book.

   A. Distribute the book to retailers.

   B. Promote the book to potential readers.

And, in actuality, the real world would often dictate that some of these subtasks be broken down even further into sub-subtasks. In any event, the starting point for using Microsoft Project 2000 to schedule tasks is to record the project's to-do list.

Identifying and Scheduling Tasks

Once you know what tasks are required to complete a project—and this may often be information you have in your head—you're ready to identify and schedule these tasks.

To identify and schedule these tasks, you take the following actions:

1. Click the first empty row in the Task Name column.

Figure 3-1 shows how the first empty row of the Task Name column looks after it's been clicked.

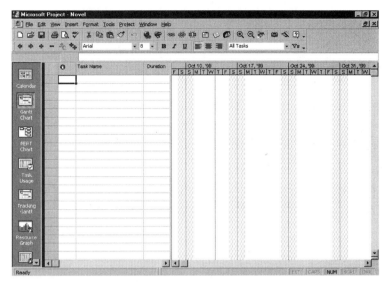

Figure 3-1   The Microsoft Project window with an empty project file.

TIP   *You can make more room for task information by dragging the bar that separates the task information area from the Gantt chart area.*

2. Enter the task description.

Type the task description. When you finish your entry, press the Tab key, press the right arrow key, or click the first empty row in the duration box.

TIP   *To make the Task Name column wider, thereby allowing more room for descriptive task names, drag the right edge of the Task Name column heading. You can also double-click the right edge of the Task Name column heading to size the column just wide enough to hold the longest task name.*

3. Estimate the task duration.

Project initially estimates the task duration as 1d, or 1 day. You can change the duration to some other value by typing the new duration value. You can also use the buttons at the right end of the Duration box to incrementally adjust the duration.

Table 3-1 lists the abbreviations available for different time measurements. You can use these as you enter the task durations.

MEASUREMENT	MEANING
m	minutes
h	hours
d	days
ed	elapsed days
w	weeks
mo	months

Table 3-1   Time abbreviations available for duration specifications.

NOTE   *Project will use the full time measurement label if there's room in the Duration column.*

Figure 3-2 shows how the project schedule looks with the first task's name entered and its duration estimated.

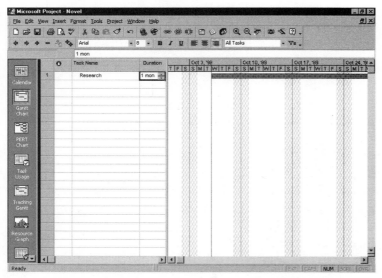

Figure 3-2   The Microsoft Project window with a task described.

4. Repeat actions 1 through 3 for the other tasks.

You need to repeat actions 1 through 3 for each of the other tasks on your to-do list. Figure 3-3 shows an example project schedule that summarizes the work required to write a book after each task is recorded.

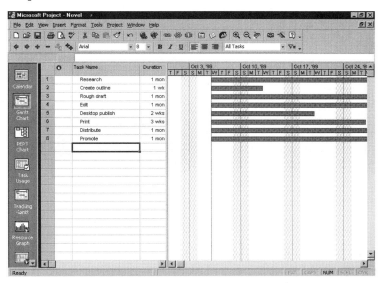

Figure 3-3   The Microsoft Project window with all the tasks on the to-do list recorded.

NOTE   *If you have a recurring task—for example, a weekly meeting—that you want to enter in a project schedule, don't enter that task following the actions described here. Instead, use the Recurring Task command described in the next section, "Recording Recurring Tasks."*

5. Optionally, add any summary tasks.

The simple project shown in Figure 3-3 is easy enough to understand because it requires only a handful of tasks. In many real-life situations, however, you will want to group tasks under summary tasks.

In the example book-publishing project, you might want to group the first four tasks under a "Write the Book" summary task, the fifth and sixth tasks under a "Print the Book" summary task, and the seventh and eighth tasks under a "Sell the Book" summary task, as shown in Figure 3-4.

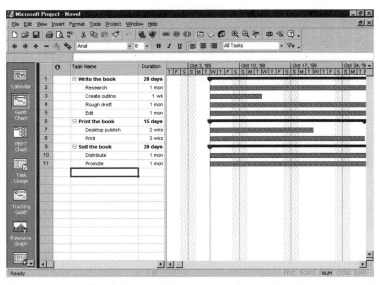

Figure 3-4   The Microsoft Project window with all summary tasks and subtasks showing.

To add summary tasks, insert a blank row above the first subtask by selecting the first subtask and then choosing the Insert menu's New Task command. Enter the summary task name in the Task Name box. Then select each of the subtasks that fall under the summary task, and click the Indent toolbar button. Figure 3-4 shows how the book-publishing project schedule looks after adding some summary tasks.

As needed, repeat the actions described in the preceding paragraph to add more summary tasks. Note that Project places any new tasks you add at the same level as the preceding task. This means that if the preceding task is a subtask, you'll want to first identify the new task as a summary task by selecting the task and then clicking the Outdent toolbar button.

NOTE   *You don't need to enter durations for summary tasks—Project determines the duration based on the critical path of the subtasks.*

Recording Recurring Tasks

You can enter most of the tasks in a project using the actions described in the preceding section. If you want to record a recurring task—a weekly meeting, monthly report, or some other regularly recurring task—you can use the Recurring Task command to enter all the recurring tasks at once.

To record recurring tasks, take the following actions:

1. **Choose the Insert menu's Recurring Tasks command.**

   Project displays the Recurring Task Information dialog box, as shown in Figure 3-5.

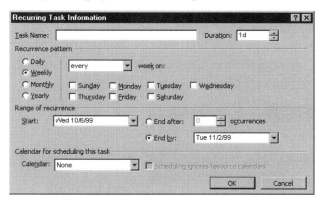

Figure 3-5   The Recurring Task Information dialog box.

2. **Enter the task description.**

   Type the task description in the Task Name box.

3. **Estimate the task duration.**

   Type a value in the Duration box to make an initial estimate of the task duration.

NOTE   *Table 3-1 lists the abbreviations available for different time measurements.*

4. **Use the Recurrence Pattern option buttons to indicate how often the task recurs.**

   When you select a Recurrence Pattern option button, Project displays additional boxes and buttons next to it that let you further define the recurrence.

   In Figure 3-5, for example, the Weekly option button is marked. Project displays boxes that let you indicate whether the task occurs every week (as opposed to, say, every other week) and on which day of the week.

5. **Use the Range Of Recurrence option buttons and boxes to indicate the length of time the task recurs.**

   You can use the Start and End By buttons and boxes to specify that the task recurs within a range of dates. Or, you can use the Start and End After buttons and boxes to specify that the task recurs a specific number of times.

6. **Click OK.**

   After you've described the recurring task, click OK. Project adds it to your project schedule.

Collecting Additional Task Information

You can use task notes to document additional task information, if necessary. For example, if you want to add assumptions implicit in scheduling some task, you might use a task note.

To add a task note to a task, double-click the task so that Project displays the Task Information dialog box as shown in Figure 3-6, and click the Notes tab.

Figure 3-6   The Notes tab of the Task Information dialog box.

To use the Notes tab, simply click inside the notes area and begin typing. You can enter information and edit information in the same way as with any scrolling text box.

The Notes tab provides a handful of formatting toolbar buttons that you can use to format your text, as described in Table 3-2.

FORMATTING TOOL	WHAT IT DOES
Format Font	Displays the Font dialog box, which you can use to choose a font, font style, and size, for the selected text.
Align Left	Left-aligns the selected text.
Center	Centers the selected text.
Align Right	Right-aligns the selected text.
Bulleted List	Turns the selected paragraphs into a bulleted list.
Insert Object	Displays the Insert Object dialog box, which you can use to insert an existing object in the note or create a new object for the note.

Table 3-2   Formatting toolbar buttons available on the Notes tab.

Fine-Tuning Duration Values

You can fine-tune the duration estimates that you provide in several ways. You can indicate that a duration is only an estimate, for example. You can also explain whether a duration depends on the passage of time or on effort.

Marking Durations as Estimates

To indicate that a duration is an estimate, double-click the task. When Project displays the Task Information dialog box, as shown in Figure 3-7, select the Estimated check box.

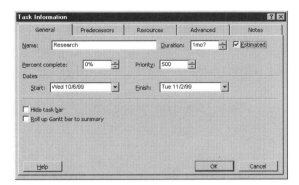

Figure 3-7   The General tab of the Task Information dialog box.

Project identifies task durations that are marked as "Estimated" by placing a question mark after the duration value, as shown in Figure 3-7.

In most cases, task durations *are* estimates. You might want to use the Estimated flag, then, to identify only a certain category of estimated durations. For example, you might use the Estimated flag to identify task durations that haven't been reviewed in relation to the resources required to complete the task.

Identifying Task Dependencies

After you list the tasks in a project, you describe the dependencies between tasks. This is simply a matter of identifying which tasks need to precede other tasks.

Returning to the example of a book-publishing project, obviously you must research the topic before you can create an outline, and you create an outline before you write the book (at least if the book is to be reasonably well organized). You must write the manuscript before you can edit and revise it, and so on.

Linking Tasks

To identify task dependencies, take the following actions:

1. Select the first task with a predecessor, or prerequisite, task.

In the example of the book-publishing project, this would be the second task listed—the task of Create Outline.

You can select a task for which you want to specify a predecessor by clicking it.

2. Identify the first predecessor of the selected task.

Click the Predecessors box for the task. Then type the task number of the predecessor task. As you identify predecessors, Project recalculates task start and finish dates

In the example of the book-publishing project, you would identify the Research task as a predecessor of the Create outline task by entering 2 in the Predecessors box of the Create Outline task, as shown in Figure 3-8.

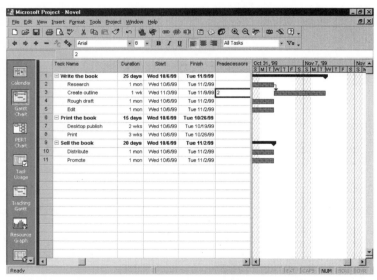

Figure 3-8   A simple book-publishing project with a predecessor task specified for the Create Outline task.

3. If necessary, identify any other predecessors of the selected task.

Some tasks require more than one predecessor. To indicate that a task requires multiple predecessors, separate the task numbers with commas. For example, to specify that both the Research and Create Outline tasks need to be completed before the Rough Draft task can start, enter 2,3 in the Rough Draft Predecessors box.

NOTE *Project assumes that a predecessor task must finish before a successor task can start. Project also assumes that as soon as the predecessor does finish, the successor can immediately start. You can tell Project to make other assumptions, however. The later section, "Understanding the Types of Dependencies," explains how to do this in its discussion of other types of predecessor-successor relationships.*

TIP *You can also link tasks in the Gantt view by selecting the names of the tasks you want to link and clicking the Link Tasks toolbar button. Alternatively, you can rest the mouse pointer over the predecessor task's bar on the Gantt chart so that it becomes a four-sided arrow. Then drag downward (but not sideways) to link the task to the successor task's bar.*

Removing Task Dependencies

To remove a task dependency, take the following actions:

1. **Select the first task with the incorrect predecessor, or prerequisite, task.**

   You can select a task for which you want to remove a predecessor by clicking it.

2. **Edit the contents of the Predecessors box.**

   Edit the incorrect predecessor task number or replace the number. You enter and edit information in a Predecessors box in the same way that you enter and edit information in any text box.

Overlapping Tasks

You have two options for specifying dependencies for tasks that partially overlap. Generally, it is best to divide the task and link the individual parts. So in the case of the book-publishing project, you could divide the writing task into individual chapters so that some of the writing could overlap with the editing. This would be a likely scenario if someone else were editing the book: you would write a few chapters and pass them off for editing as you continued to write. However, for tasks that aren't easily divisible, you can also include lead-time between the tasks. To do so, take the following actions:

1. **Double-click the dependent task.**

   Project displays the Task Information dialog box for the task.

2. Click the Predecessors tab.

Figure 3-9 shows the Predecessors tab of the Task Information dialog box.

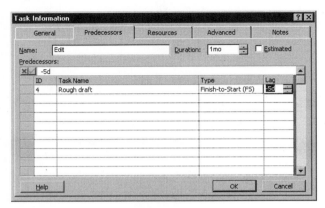

Figure 3-9   Making tasks overlap.

3. Specify the overlap between tasks using the Lag box.

Either enter a negative value in the Lag box or click the down arrow on the right side of the Lag box to reduce the lag from the default of 0.

Adding Lag Time

Some projects require lag time between tasks. For example, if your task is baking a loaf of bread, you need to somehow represent the time it takes for the bread to rise after you knead it. You have two options for doing this. Generally, the best idea is to create a separate task for this lag. So for a bread-baking project, you would include an hour-long Let Rise task. However, you could also add a lag between the Kneading task and the task that comes after letting the bread rise, namely punching down the dough. To do so, you would double-click the Punch Down Dough task, click the Predecessors tab, and enter 60m in the Lag box.

Understanding the Types of Dependencies

Most tasks link so that the start of one task begins after the finish of another. However, Project offers a few other dependency types. Table 3-3 describes these other dependency types and offers examples of when they are used.

DEPENDENCY	USED FOR
Start-to-Finish (SF)	When the start of the successor task drives the timing of the end of the predecessor task. For example, if you make improvements to a production facility, closing it temporarily, you want to shut down the backup facility only when the main production facility can resume operations.
Start-to-Start (SS)	When two tasks must start at the same time. For example, you need two resources to meet and grant approval for two processes to begin as soon as possible. If one person is delayed, you need to delay the start of both tasks.
Finish-to-Finish (FF)	When the end of tasks should be linked so they finish at exactly the same time. For example, if you make two improvements to a building that require inspection by a service that charges an expensive per-visit fee, you want to make sure that both improvements finish at the same time so they can be inspected in one visit. If one finishes later, then the other must as well so that the inspection visit can be rescheduled.

Table 3-3   Dependency types available in Project.

To set the type of dependency, double-click the task and click the Predecessors tab in the Task Information dialog box. Then select a dependency type from the Type drop-down list box.

NOTE   *You can set dependency types only in the Task Information dialog box. If you link tasks using the Link Tasks toolbar button or by dragging between taskbars in the Gantt chart, Project assumes that the tasks should link finish-to-start.*

Adding Other Scheduling Goals and Constraints

For many tasks, you don't need to do more than provide a name and the duration and then list the predecessor tasks. However, you may want to identify important project milestones—perhaps so you can more easily report project progress to stakeholders. In some cases, you may also want to more accurately describe any scheduling constraints.

Adding Milestones

One common project-management convention is to add milestones to the project. A milestone represents a marker that project stakeholders can use to assess progress.

To add a milestone to a project, click the task below the task upon which you want to base the milestone. Choose the Insert menu's New Task command. When Project displays the Task Information dialog box, use it to give the milestone a name. Specify the duration as 0. Indicate which task is a predecessor to the milestone task.

Repeat the sequence of actions described in the preceding paragraph to add additional milestones as necessary.

Figure 3-10 shows two milestones added to the example of the book-publishing project: "Manuscript complete" and "Book printed."

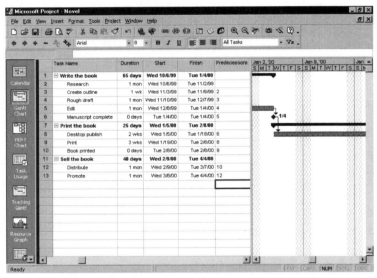

Figure 3-10   The Microsoft Project window with two milestones.

NOTE   *You don't have to use milestones. You can use important tasks—or their completion dates—as markers for monitoring progress.*

Adding Constraint Dates

Project lets you add two scheduling constraints to your project: deadlines, before which a task must be completed, and constraint types, which let you indicate scheduling characteristics such as the fact that a task should start as soon as possible or as late as possible.

To add either scheduling constraint to a task, take the following actions:

1. Double-click the task.

Project opens the Task Information dialog box, as shown in Figure 3-11.

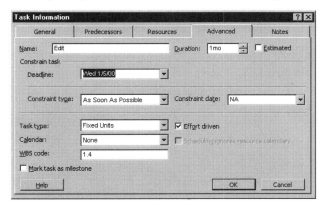

Figure 3-11 The Task Information dialog box with the Advanced tab showing a deadline.

2. Specify a deadline, if necessary.

If a task must be completed by a specific date, enter this date in the Deadline box.

When you specify a deadline, Project compares the estimated finish date for a task to the deadline. If the estimated finish date falls after the deadline, Project alerts you to this problem by flagging the task in the Gantt view with an exclamation mark.

3. Specify a starting or ending date constraint, if necessary.

By default, Project schedules tasks to start as soon as possible but only after any predecessor tasks are complete.

You can change this scheduling rule by choosing a constraint from the Constraint Type drop-down list box. For example, you can indicate that Project should schedule some task to start as late as possible but without delaying the projected completion date. (To do this, you choose the As Late As Possible entry from the Constraint Type list box.)

The Constraint Type list box also provides a series of self-explanatory constraints that let you indicate that a task should start or finish by a specified date. For example, you can specify that a task must start by a particular date. To specify this date, you use the Constraint Date box.

NOTE   *Although adding constraint dates to tasks often complicates a schedule, such constraints are sometimes necessary. For example, a contract may state that some task must be started or finished by a specific date.*

Resolving Dependency-Constraint Conflicts

When you specify constraint dates, you often create conflicts between dependencies and constraint dates. Suppose, for example, that task B can start only after task A finishes and that task A finishes on June 1. If you set a constraint date that says task B must start on May 1, your dependency and constraint date conflict.

Project looks for and alerts you to any dependency-constraint conflicts. To notify you, Project displays a series of Planning Wizard dialog boxes that warn you about the possible effects of your scheduling constraint and ask you to confirm that by using such a constraint you know you're overriding Project's date calculations, as shown in Figure 3-12.

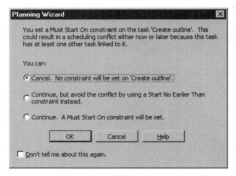

Figure 3-12   The Planning Wizard alerts you to a dependency-constraint conflict.

The Planning Wizard dialog box gives you choices as to how you can deal with a dependency-constraint conflict. One way is simply to cancel the creation of a dependency or constraint that creates the conflict. You do this by selecting the Cancel—No Constraint Will Be Set option button and then clicking OK.

Another way to deal with the dependency-constraint conflict is to acknowledge the conflict—but then tell Project to ignore the conflict. You do this by selecting the Continue—But Avoid The Conflict option button.

Project "fixes" a scheduling conflict by ignoring the dependency and using only the constraint date in its scheduling. Which means, of course, that you need to be very careful about how you use these scheduling exceptions because scheduling exceptions usually override the basic logic of a schedule.

Project may also suggest a "flexible constraint;" in this example a Start No Earlier Than constraint. The task is constrained to the specified date, unless the linked task forces this task's dates to change. The linked task still takes precedence over the task's dates.

The flexible constraints Project suggests will differ, depending on the type of constraint you attempt to use, and whether your project is scheduled from the start date or the finish date.

If you don't want Project to fix scheduling constraints by overriding dependencies and focusing exclusively on the constraint date, take the following actions:

1. Choose the Tools menu's Options command, and click the Schedule tab.

Project displays the Schedule tab of the Options dialog box, as shown in Figure 3-13.

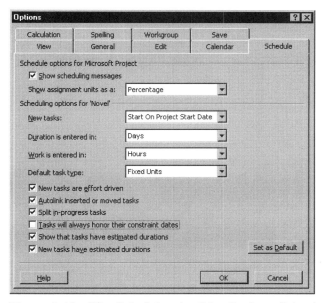

Figure 3-13   The Schedule tab of the Options dialog box.

2. Clear the Tasks Will Always Honor Their Constraint Dates check box.

After you've made this specification, click OK. Project closes the dialog box.

Summary

After you've identified and scheduled your project tasks, taking into account task dependencies and constraints, you've actually accomplished the first of the two major planning steps related to organizing a project. The second major planning step is described in "Step 4: Identify and Allocate Resources."

IDENTIFY AND ALLOCATE RESOURCES

Tasks Required to Complete the Step

- Allocating resources
- Fine-tuning duration calculations for resources
- Creating different calendars for groups of resources
- Editing calendars for individual resources
- Reviewing resource allocations
- Leveling resources
- Assigning costs to resources
- Sharing resources

For most projects, you need to assign and then monitor resources such as people and equipment. This is the fourth step in managing a project using Microsoft Project 2000.

Allocating Resources

In simple situations, you can easily identify and assign resources to a project. Take the case of the project shown in Figure 4-1, for example. You can simultaneously identify and allocate resources simply by entering resource names in the Resource Names column of the Gantt chart.

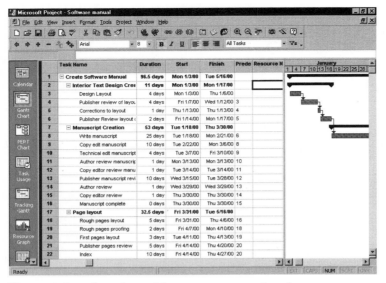

Figure 4-1   A project without resources assigned.

Assigning Resources

To assign resources to tasks, take the following actions:

1. Select the task to which you want to assign a resource.

To do this most easily, simply click the Resource Names box of the task.

2. Name the resource.

To do this, type the resource name or a short description. You might, for example, use a person's first name if you have only a short list of people resources: Alice, Bob, Carmen, and so on.

If your project requires the efforts of many people, you might use first initials in combination with last names: Dellington, Nbonaparte, and so on.

If a task requires more than one resource, separate resource names with commas, as shown in Figure 4-2.

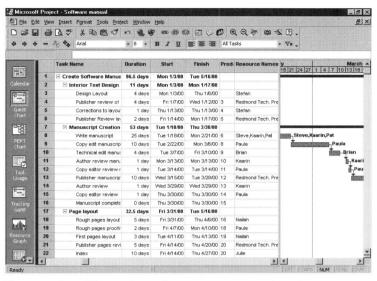

Figure 4-2   The project after resources are assigned.

NOTE   *Resources also include any equipment or machinery your project requires, such as a bulldozer, a helicopter, or a crane, as described in detail in the next section.*

3. Repeat actions 1 and 2 for each task to which you want to assign resources.

You should presumably assign resources to all tasks and subtasks, but not milestones and not summary tasks. As a practical matter, resource allocations often represent guesses on your part until you can confirm that a resource is available.

Specifying Parts and Equipment as Resources

As mentioned earlier, not only can you add human resources to tasks, but you can also assign materials and equipment to tasks. To do so, enter the material or equipment for the task in the Resource Names column of the Gantt chart in the same way that you enter a human resource. Then take the following actions:

1. Click the Resource Sheet icon on the View Bar.

Project displays the Resource Sheet listing the project's resources.

2. Click the Type column for the material resource, and select Material from the drop-down list box.

3. Press the Enter key.

Project displays a message box alerting you that you're changing the resource type.

4. Click OK.

Project adjusts the columns of the Resource Sheet to make them appropriate for costs of goods rather than services, as shown in Figure 4-3.

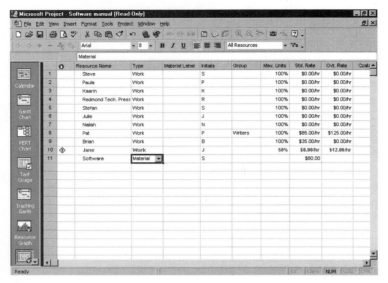

Figure 4-3   Adding a material good as a resource.

5. In the Material Label column, enter the units by which you'll specify the value required.

For example, if you enter fuel as a material resource, you would enter gallons or liters.

6. Specify the cost of the good.

If you're paying rent to use the good, enter a value in the Std. Rate column. If the good costs a flat fee, enter the cost in the Cost/Use column.

NOTE   *If your project uses a currency for cost amounts different from the currency settings described in the Regional Settings tool on your computer, choose the Tools menu's Options command and click the View tab. Then enter the currency symbol your project uses and the number of decimal digits, and specify the placement of the symbol in regard to the value. For example, if your project costs are in German marks, you would enter DM (for Deutsche mark) in the Symbol box and select 1 DM from the Placement drop-down list box.*

7. **When you're finished, click the Gantt Chart icon on the View Bar to return to the Gantt chart.**

   Project places the value 1 in square brackets after the good's name in the Resource Names column, assuming that the quantity of the good required for the task is one. To specify a different quantity, change the value in the square brackets.

Removing Resources

You can easily remove resources you've assigned. One simple way to do this is to clear the Resource Names box shown in the Gantt Chart view. To do so, select the Resource Names box, select the resource's name from the Entry bar (located at the top of the Gantt chart and Task Name list) or click the Resource Names box again, select the resource's name, and press the Delete key. Figure 4-4 shows a resource name selected in the Entry bar.

WARNING   *Don't just select the Resource Names box and press the Delete key. This deletes the entire task.*

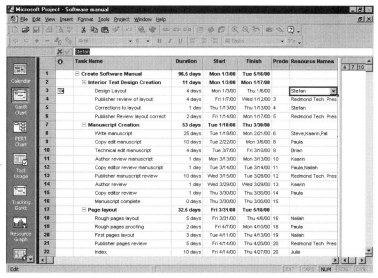

Figure 4-4   You can remove a resource by clearing or editing the name in the Resource Names box by using the Entry bar.

You can also remove a resource from a task using the Assign Resources command. To use this command, take the following actions:

1. Click the Assign Resources toolbar button.

You can also choose the Tools menu's Resources command and then choose the submenu's Assign Resources command. After you click the toolbar button or choose the command, Project displays the Assign Resources dialog box, as shown in Figure 4-5.

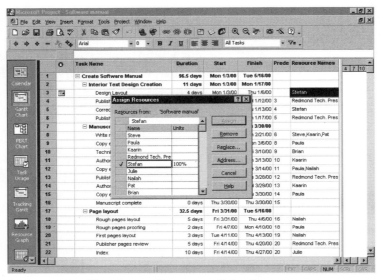

Figure 4-5 The Assign Resources dialog box.

NOTE *The Assign Resources toolbar button shows two faces in profile. Note, too, that if you point to the Assign Resources toolbar button, Project displays the button's name in a pop-up box called a ScreenTip.*

2. Select the task for which you want to remove a resource.

You can do this by clicking the task in the Gantt Chart view, which appears beneath the Assign Resources dialog box.

3. Select the assigned resource you want to remove.

Using the list box of resources shown in the Assign Resources dialog box, select the resource you want to remove by clicking it. To select more than one resource, press and hold down the Ctrl key and then click each resource.

4. Click the Remove button.

When you click Remove, Project removes each of the selected resources from the selected task. To close the dialog box, click its Close box.

Making Resource Substitutions

You can replace resources using the Assign Resources command and its dialog box. To use the Assign Resources command and dialog box for this purpose, take the following actions:

1. **Click the Assign Resources toolbar button.**

   Again, you can also choose the Tools menu's Resources command and then choose the submenu's Assign Resources command. After you click the toolbar button or choose the command, Project displays the Assign Resources dialog box, as shown in Figure 4-6.

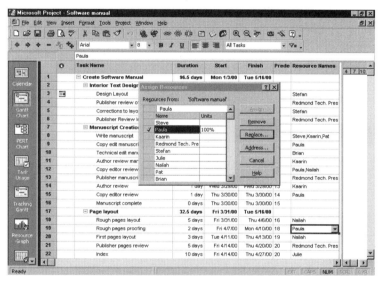

Figure 4-6 The Assign Resources dialog box.

2. **Select the task for which you want to substitute a resource.**

   You can do this by clicking the task in the Gantt Chart view, which appears beneath the Assign Resources dialog box.

3. **Select the assigned resource you want to replace.**

   Using the list box of resources shown in the Assign Resources dialog box, select the resource you want to replace by clicking it.

   To select more than one resource, press and hold down the Ctrl key and then click each resource.

4. Click the Replace button.

When you click Replace, Project displays the Replace Resource dialog box, as shown in Figure 4-7.

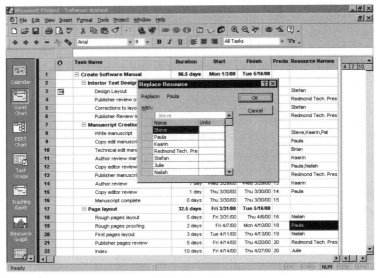

Figure 4-7   The Replace Resource dialog box.

5. Select the new replacement resource.

Using the list box of resources shown in the Replace Resource dialog box, select the resource you want to substitute by clicking it.

6. Replace the resource.

With the Replace Resource dialog box displayed, click OK. Project replaces the resource and redisplays the Assign Resources dialog box. To close the dialog box, click its Close box.

Fine-Tuning Duration Calculations for Resources

By default, when you specify a task duration in Project, Project assumes the task requires a specified amount of effort. If you indicate that some task will take four days, Project assumes you mean the task requires four days of work, or effort. Project calls effort-based durations *fixed-unit durations*. Tasks with fixed-unit durations are called *fixed-unit tasks*.

With fixed-unit tasks, adding more resources results in the task finishing more quickly. Suppose, for example, that a fixed unit task has a four-day duration. With one person assigned to the task, the task takes four days to complete. With two people assigned, the task takes two days to complete. With four people, one day.

In addition to fixed-unit durations, Project lets you specify two other types of duration: *fixed duration* and *fixed work*.

A fixed-duration task indicates that the passage of time itself is required. In a construction project, for example, concrete may actually require the passage of time in order to cure. If you indicate that a concrete foundation requires four days to cure, the task Cure concrete takes four days no matter what resources you assign.

A fixed-work task amounts to a hybrid of fixed-unit tasks and fixed-duration tasks. With a fixed-work task, you can't accelerate the task's completion by adding resources. But as you add resources, you reduce the percentage of the resource devoted to the task. For example, if a fixed-work task has a duration of four days and you assign one person, the task requires all, or 100%, of the person's time for four days. If you assign two people, however, while the project still takes four days to complete, it requires only half, or 50%, of the people's time over those four days. If you assign four people, the project still takes four days, but it now requires only one quarter, or 25%, of the people's time.

To specify how Project should calculate the duration for some task, take the following actions:

1. **Double-click the task.**

   Project opens the Task Information dialog box. Click the Advanced tab to show the Advanced tab of options, as shown in Figure 4-8.

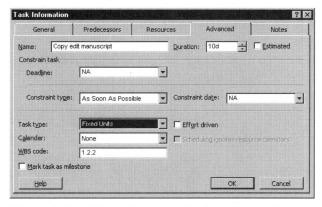

Figure 4-8   The Advanced tab of the Task Information dialog box.

2. **Select the appropriate duration calculation method.**

Open the Task Type drop-down list box. Select the appropriate duration calculation method from the Task Type drop-down list box: Fixed Units (the default), Fixed Duration, or Fixed Work.

3. **Indicate whether Project should recalculate the time it takes to complete the task or the effort assigned to the task.**

Select or clear the Effort Driven check box to indicate whether Project should calculate the duration based on the effort or the effort based on the duration.

NOTE   *A fixed-work task is by definition effort driven, so the Effort Driven check box is always selected for this duration calculation method. You have the option of clearing the Effort Driven check box only for fixed-duration or fixed-unit tasks.*

The Effort Driven check box's effect can seem confusing at first, but it follows these rules to adjust the duration and effort:

- If the Effort Driven check box is selected for a fixed-unit task, Project recalculates the task duration when you change the resources assigned to the task, but Project doesn't recalculate the resources assigned to the task when you change the duration.

- If the Effort Driven check box is *not* selected for a fixed-unit task, Project recalculates the task duration when you change the resources assigned to the task and recalculates the resources assigned to the task when you change the duration.

- If the Effort Driven check box is selected for a fixed-duration task, Project recalculates the resources assigned to the task when you change the resources assigned to the task, but Project doesn't recalculate the duration when you change the resources and it doesn't recalculate the resources assigned to the task when you change the duration.

- If the Effort Driven check box is *not* selected for a fixed-duration task, Project doesn't recalculate the resources assigned to the task when you change the resources assigned to the task, and it doesn't recalculate the duration when you change the resources assigned to the task.

To specify that a resource will work only part-time on a task, take the following actions:

1. Display the project in Gantt Chart view.

If necessary, click the Gantt Chart button on the View Bar to display the project in Gantt Chart view.

2. Select the Resource Names column for the task to which you want to assign part-time resources.

Project displays any resources you've assigned to the task in the Entry bar at the top of the Gantt chart and Task Name list.

3. After a resource's name, enter the percentage of time the resource will work on the task in square brackets.

Do not leave a space between the resource's name and the brackets. Figure 4-9 shows a resource assigned to work on a task for 40% of a full day's work as specified by the project's calendar. If you specified the task as Fixed Units or Fixed Work, Project recalculates the task duration.

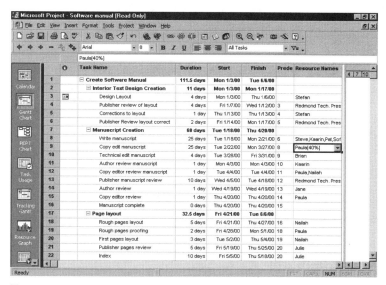

Figure 4-9   Specifying that a resource works part-time on a task.

Creating Different Calendars for Groups of Resources

Step 2 describes how to create a base calendar for a project or the company. However, if you have groups of resources working different schedules, you may want to create specific calendars for these groups and assign the resources to the calendars. For example, you might have a group of resources on assignment and unavailable for a certain month of the year. Likewise, you might have people working in international divisions who celebrate different holidays and work different schedules.

NOTE   *Create new base calendars only for groups of resources who share similar schedules, not for individuals. The section "Editing Calendars for Individual Resources" later in this step describes how you can personalize calendars for individuals.*

To create a new calendar for a group of resources, take the following actions:

1. **Choose the Tools menu's Change Working Time command.**

   Project displays the Change Working Time dialog box, as shown in Figure 4-10.

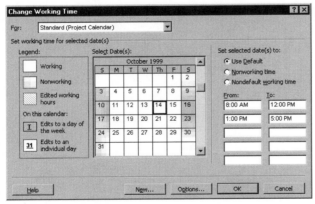

Figure 4-10   The Change Working Time dialog box.

2. **Indicate you want to create a new calendar.**

   Click the New button. Project displays the Create New Base Calendar dialog box, as shown in Figure 4-11.

Figure 4-11 The Create New Base Calendar dialog box.

3. Name the new base calendar.

Enter the name you want to use for the project calendar. For example, you might enter *Seasonal crew* or *Frankfurt division*.

4. Copy an existing schedule's information as a starting point.

Click the Make A Copy Of option button, select one of the existing calendars of working and nonworking time from the drop-down list box, and then click OK.

5. Identify nonworking days.

To identify nonworking days not already included on the base calendar, use the calendar shown in the Change Working Time dialog box to display the month with the holidays. After the month shows, press and hold down the Ctrl key and click each day that you want to mark as a nonworking day.

6. Describe exceptions to the typical workday or workweek.

To identify any exceptions to the typical workday or workweek, use the calendar shown in the Change Working Time dialog box to show the month with the exceptions.

After the month shows, press and hold down the Ctrl key and click each of the days with the exception.

After you do this, click the Nondefault Working Time option button and use the From and To boxes to describe the exception.

NOTE *The Change Working Time dialog box provides a legend explaining how working, nonworking, and nondefault working times appear on the calendar.*

7. Save your calendar.

Click OK to save your calendar changes.

8. Attach resources to the correct calendar.

Display the Resource Sheet and scroll over to the Base Calendar column. Select the correct base calendar for each resource, as shown in Figure 4-12.

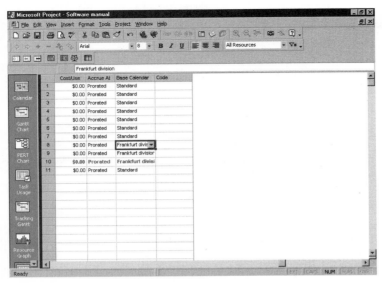

Figure 4-12 Selecting the correct base calendar for each resource.

Editing Calendars for Individual Resources

By default, Project uses your base calendars for showing resource availability. If the base calendar shows that June 1 is a working day, Project assumes that the resources to whom that calendar applies are available on June 1. If the project calendar shows that June 1 is a nonworking day, Project assumes that resources aren't available that day.

Sometimes, however, you need to edit a calendar specifically for an individual resource. For instance, you can edit a calendar to show when a specific human resource goes on vacation or takes a leave of absence. In essence, you'll create a resource calendar by making a copy of the base calendar and then making any needed changes.

NOTE   *If you don't want to edit calendars for individual resources, you can also manu-*
ally organize your projects in such a way that you don't rely on a worker the
same week she is on vacation or on a piece of machinery the same week it's
being serviced.

To customize a calendar for a particular resource, take the following actions:

1. Display the Resource Sheet.

Choose the View menu's Resource Sheet command. Or, alternatively, click the Resource Sheet icon on the View Bar. Project displays the Resource Sheet, as shown in Figure 4-13.

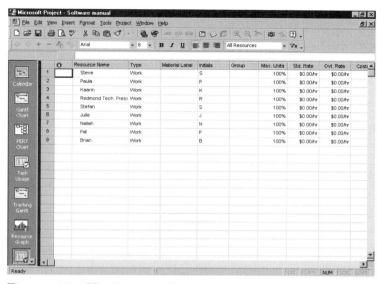

Figure 4-13   The Resource Sheet.

2. Double-click the resource.

Project displays the Resource Information dialog box for the resource. Click the Working Time tab to display the set of options shown in Figure 4-14.

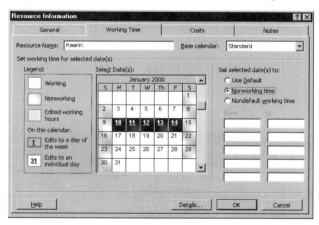

Figure 4-14   The Working Time tab of the Resource Information dialog box.

3. Verify the resource's base calendar.

Use the Base Calendar drop-down list to select the calendar that most closely matches the resource's schedule.

4. **Identify the resource's nonworking days.**

To identify nonworking days, such as vacation and personal leave days, use the calendar shown on the Working Time tab. You can move backward or forward in the calendar by dragging the slider on the vertical scroll bar on the right side of the calendar.

After the month shows, press and hold down the Ctrl key and click each day that you want to mark as a nonworking day.

After you've done this, click the Nonworking Time option button. Figure 4-14 shows the second week of January 2000 marked as nonworking days.

5. **Describe exceptions to the typical workday or workweek.**

To identify any exceptions to the typical workday or workweek, use the calendar to display the month with the exception. Then press and hold down the Ctrl key and click each of the days with the exception.

After you do this, click the Nondefault Working Time option button and use the From and To boxes to describe the exception. Figure 4-15 shows May 31, 2000, as a four-hour workday, which is an exception to the typical eight-hour workday.

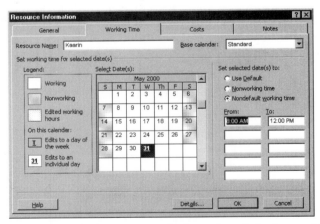

Figure 4-15   The Resource Information dialog box—this time showing an exception to the usual eight-hour workday.

NOTE   *The Resource Information dialog box provides a legend explaining how work-ing, nonworking, and nondefault working times appear on the calendar.*

6. If necessary, specify the worker as seasonal or part-time.

Click the General tab of the Resource Information dialog box. Use the Available From and Available To boxes to specify the range of dates the resource is available. Use the Units box to specify the amount of the resource available as a percentage. For example, 50% would be a half-time resource, 67% would be a two-thirds time resource. Figure 4-16 shows the General tab of the Resource Information dialog box filled out for a high school student.

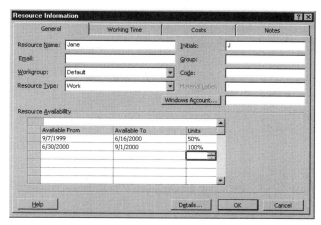

Figure 4-16   Specifying worker availability.

7. Save your calendar changes.

Click OK to save your resource calendar changes.

8. Repeat actions 2 through 6, as necessary.

To create resource calendars for other resources, repeat actions 2 through 6 as necessary.

Reviewing Resource Allocations

After you allocate resources and, if necessary, verify that Project's duration calculations are working correctly, you should review the allocations.

Obviously, you want to make sure that people aren't overscheduled. Overtime, apart from the personal burden it places on team members, also creates project risks because it means there's never any cushion in people's schedules.

You also often want to make sure that people stay busy. A schedule in which someone works sporadically doesn't work well for the individual or for the project.

Using the Resource Sheet View

Often, you can most easily review the resource allocations you've made by using the Resource Sheet view, as shown in Figure 4-17. To view a Resource Sheet for the open project file, choose the View menu's Resource Sheet command or click the Resource Sheet button on the View Bar.

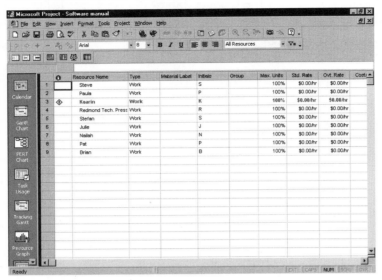

Figure 4-17 The Resource Sheet.

NOTE *Project identifies any overallocated resources by placing an exclamation point in the Indicator column of the Resource Sheet. On your monitor, Project also flags these overallocated resources by displaying them in red.*

Using the Resource Graph View

Another handy view is the Resource Graph, shown in Figure 4-18. It shows resource usage in a bar chart, depicting regular hours in blue (on a color monitor or printer) and overtime hours in red. To view a Resource Graph for the open project file, choose the View menu's Resource Graph command or click the Resource Graph button on the View Bar.

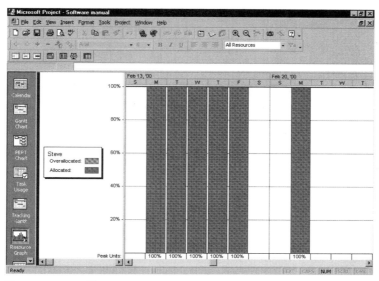

Figure 4-18 The Resource Graph.

To scroll through the resources, slide the scroll bar in the left area of the Resource Graph view. This area names the resource depicted in the Resource Graph.

To scroll through the calendar, slide the scroll bar in the right area of the Resource Graph view. This area shows the bar chart of resource allocation.

Using the Resource Usage View

Still one other view that depicts resources is the Resource Usage view, shown in Figure 4-19. It shows resource usage in a table by task. To view a Resource Usage view for the open project file, choose the View menu's Resource Usage command or click the Resource Usage button on the View Bar.

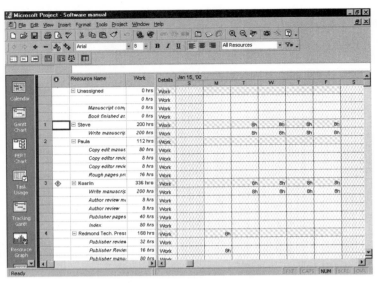

Figure 4-19 The Resource Usage view.

NOTE *To collapse the tasks detail for a resource so that only the resource's total assigned hours show, click the button marked with the minus (-) symbol. To later expand the tasks, click the button marked with the plus (+) symbol. Project replaces the minus button with the plus button and vice versa when you click it.*

Leveling Resources

Many projects show overallocated resources—yet without creating problems. Slightly overscheduled resources can sometimes work overtime. Other times, despite what the schedule shows, the project still stays on track even if work slides around a little: Work that the schedule shows should be done on Tuesday through Thursday can instead be spread from Monday through Friday, for example.

When the resource overallocation isn't acceptable, you have two recourses: You can adjust the schedule manually by adding resources, reducing durations, or eliminating constraints. Or, you can tell Project to level resources. Resource leveling stretches out the project schedule so that resource overallocation is eliminated.

Leveling Resources Manually

Manual resource leveling works the way you would expect. Your first action may be to review first-guess durations as well as any constraints to see whether durations can be tightened and constraints loosened. Either sort of change can easily fix overallocations.

Your second action may be to look at assigning more resources. Instead of using one person, you might try two. Or three. Commonly, you lose efficiency at some point. But still, assigning a team of people is often possible.

To reduce resource overallocation by assigning multiple resources, the task duration type must be set to either Fixed Units or Fixed Work and Effort Driven.

NOTE *For more information about these two types of duration, see the earlier section, "Fine-Tuning Duration Calculations for Resources."*

Still a third technique for leveling resources is to reorganize the project so the work of a resource is spread over a greater length of time. In computer book publishing, for example, we actually do this by breaking tasks into subtasks (and sometimes breaking subtasks into sub-subtasks). This gambit often lets a resource begin work earlier and finish work later than would otherwise be possible because work can be done concurrently.

For example, in most book publishing, a book is written and then it is edited. If writing takes three months and editing takes two months and the editing task must follow the writing task, the project duration equals five months.

In computer book publishing, however, as a writer finishes an individual chapter (or perhaps a set of chapters), the chapters go to the editor for editing. In this manner, work is scheduled concurrently. As the writer is writing chapter 3, say, the editor is editing chapters 1 and 2.

You can use this concurrent scheduling to reduce the time it takes to finish a project, of course. You can also use this concurrent scheduling to finish the project in the same length of time as originally scheduled—except with resource usage spread over longer periods of time.

NOTE *For more information about dividing and linking tasks, refer to "Step 3: Schedule Project Tasks."*

Leveling Resources Automatically

Automatic resource leveling stretches out the project by delaying tasks and splitting tasks. When Project delays a task, it simply moves it into the future when the resource is available. When it splits a task, work on the task progresses at various intervals—but only when resources are available.

Limits exist, however, as to what Project will do as it levels resources. Project won't violate any constraints you've set as it levels resources, for example.

NOTE *For more information about constraints, refer to the section "Adding Other Scheduling Goals and Constraints" in "Step 3: Schedule Project Tasks."*

Project also won't delay or split any tasks to which you've assigned a priority of 1000. In other words, you use the priority setting of 1000 to show that a task shouldn't be adjusted in any resource leveling.

NOTE *To set a task priority to 1000 so that it won't be adjusted, double-click the task in the Gantt Chart view (or some other view) to display the Task Information dialog box. Then click the General tab, and enter 1000 in the Priority box.*

To level the resources in a project, take the following actions:

1. Choose the Tools menu's Resource Leveling command.

Project displays the Resource Leveling dialog box, as shown in Figure 4-20.

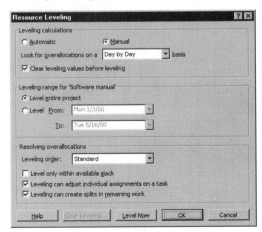

Figure 4-20   The Resource Leveling dialog box.

2. **Choose either Automatic or Manual resource leveling.**

   You can direct Project to either automatically level resources as you work or to level resources only when you choose the Resource Leveling command.

   To make this choice, click the appropriate button: Automatic or Manual.

   NOTE   *Automatic resource leveling is calculation-intense for Project and your personal computer. For large or complex projects, this option may noticeably slow down Project's speed and responsiveness.*

3. **Indicate the time interval at which Project should watch for overallocation.**

   You use the Look For Overallocations drop-down list box to specify, essentially, just what an overallocation is. Is a resource overallocated if it's scheduled for more than eight hours in a day? Forty hours in a week? Sixty minutes in an hour?

   By default, Project considers any day in which a resource is scheduled for more than a full day's work (probably eight hours) as a resource overallocation. In this case, the Look For Overallocations box shows Day By Day.

   It may be, however, that you can work with a looser definition of overallocation. For example, if an overallocation doesn't really occur unless a resource is scheduled for more than a full week's work in a week, you might select Week By Week.

   The Look For Overallocations drop-down list box also provides even looser definitions of overallocations (like Month By Month) as well as tighter definitions of overallocation (Hour By Hour and Minute By Minute).

   NOTE   *The looser the definition you use for overallocation, the less resource leveling Project performs.*

4. **Optionally, select a range of dates for which Project should level resources.**

   If the Level Entire Project option button is selected—which is the default setting—Project will level resources over the entire project schedule.

   You can also limit Project's leveling to a specified period of time. To do this, select the Level option button and then define the range of dates using the From and To boxes.

5. **Specify the order in which Project should consider leveling criteria.**

   The Leveling Order drop-down list box provides three leveling order options: ID Only, Standard, and Priority/Standard.

The default leveling order is Standard. In this case, Project levels tasks by considering first their predecessor dependencies, then their slack, and then their dates, priorities, and constraints.

If you select ID Only, Project levels tasks in ascending ID number order and then, if that's not enough, goes on to include other leveling considerations, including predecessor dependencies, slack, dates, priorities, and constraints.

If you select Priority/Standard, Project first considers the task priorities, then predecessor dependencies, and then slack, dates, and constraints.

6. **Indicate whether Project can move the finish date.**

   If Project can or can't move the finish, or project completion, date, select the Level Only Within Available Slack check box. With this box marked, Project will perform minor adjustments, but it won't do anything that delays a path on the critical path.

7. **Indicate whether Project can individually adjust when a resource works on a task.**

   If Project can individually adjust when a resource works on a task—independent of the work that other resources working on the same task perform—select the Leveling Can Adjust Individual Assignments On A Task check box.

8. **Indicate whether Project can split a task so it occurs at two or more separate times.**

   If Project can split a task so it occurs at different times, select the Leveling Can Create Splits In Remaining Work check box.

9. **Start leveling.**

   After you've described how Project should level the resources, click the Level Now button. Project levels the project's resources.

Undoing Your Resource Leveling

You can reverse the effects of Project's resource leveling in either of two ways: If you've just leveled resources and haven't made other changes to the project, you can choose the Edit menu's Undo Leveling command.

If you've made changes to the project since leveling resources, you can choose the Tools menu's Resource Leveling command. Then, when Project displays the Resource Leveling dialog box, click the Clear Leveling button.

Assigning Costs to Resources

To assign costs to resources, take the following actions:

1. Display the Resource Sheet.

Choose the View menu's Resource Sheet command. Or, alternatively, click the Resource Sheet button on the View Bar. Project displays the Resource Sheet.

2. Double-click the resource.

When Project displays the Resource Information dialog box, click the Costs tab shown in Figure 4-21.

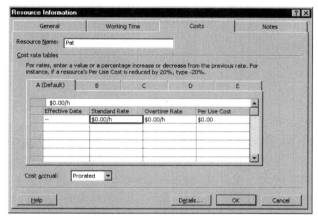

Figure 4-21 The Costs tab in the Resource Information dialog box before providing cost information.

3. Create a cost rate table for the resource.

Describe the cost of the resource by providing the standard hourly rate, an overtime rate, and, if appropriate, any one-time cost or charge associated simply with using the resource.

If a resource's costs will change at some point in the future, you can also provide this information by adding an effective date and then new standard hourly, overtime hourly, and one-time cost information.

Figure 4-22 shows the A cost rate schedule for resource "Pat." Through July 1, 2000, the resource's standard cost is $85 per hour, $125 per overtime hour. After July 1, 2000, the resource's standard cost increases to $100 an hour, and the overtime cost increases to $150 an hour.

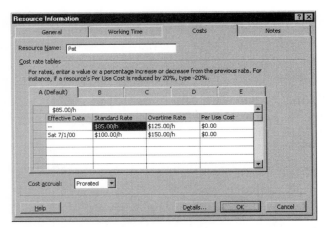

Figure 4-22 The Resource Information dialog box after providing cost information.

TIP *To describe a standard rate for resources, choose the Tools menu's Options command and click the General tab. Enter the standard rates in the Default Standard Rate and Default Overtime Rate boxes.*

4. Optionally, repeat step 3 to create additional cost rate tables.

Project lets you create more than one cost rate table for a resource. Many times, you won't need or want to do this. If you have a resource that produces different costs depending on how it is used, you might choose to set up a separate cost rate table for each type of use.

An attorney who does both legal research and provides expert testimony, for example, might charge different rates for each type of service. To deal with this, you could use two cost rate tables.

To create another cost rate table, click the next cost rate table tab, and then use it to describe the other cost rate.

5. Use the Cost Accrual drop-down list box to specify how and when you want resource costs charged to a task.

Select Start to calculate the cost for the task as soon as the task begins. Select End to calculate the cost when the task is completed, or select Prorated to accrue the cost of the task as the work is completed.

NOTE *If you set a Per Use Cost for a resource, Project always adds this cost to the task at the start of the task.*

6. **Describe the other resources in the project, as necessary.**

Repeat actions 2 through 4 to describe each of the other resources in the project.

TIP   *You can also assign a single cost rate table to a resource directly on the Resource Sheet. Just enter values in the Std. Rate, Ovt. Rate, and Cost/Use columns.*

Sharing Resources

If you have several projects (or anticipate additional projects) and want to use a common group of resources for them, you can create a resource pool to share the resources across projects. The convenience of a resource pool is that you enter information about the individual resources only once. Depending on the amount of resource information you enter, creating a shared resource pool can save you a lot of time.

Setting Up a Resource Pool

To set up a resource pool, take the following actions:

1. **Create or save a Project file that contains resource information.**

If you have already created a project that contains the information about the resources, open it and save it under a new name. (You don't need to delete the tasks.) If you haven't created a project that contains the resource information you want to share, do so.

NOTE   *Although you technically don't need to create a separate Project file for the resource pool, it usually makes sense to do so, especially in a multi-user environment. Otherwise, when you want to edit the project containing the resource pool, you block others out of working with projects linked to the resource pool.*

2. **Open the Project file that you want to link to the resource pool.**

Either create a new project or open an existing project.

3. **Choose the Tools menu's Resources command, and choose the submenu's Share Resources command.**

Project displays the Share Resources dialog box, as shown in Figure 4-23.

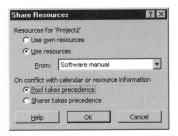

Figure 4-23   The Share Resources dialog box.

4. Specify the file with the resource pool.

Click the Use Resources option button, and select the file with the resource pool from the From drop-down list box.

5. Specify what Project should do if it encounters calendar conflicts.

Click the Pool Takes Precedence option button to make the calendars in the resource pool file take precedence. Click the Sharer Takes Precedence option button to make the calendars in the active Project file take precedence.

6. Click OK.

Project links the file to the resource pool.

Using a Project File with a Shared Resource Pool

When you later open the project that uses the resource pool, Project displays the Open Resource Pool Information dialog box, as shown in Figure 4-24.

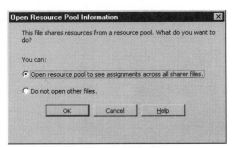

Figure 4-24   The Open Resource Pool Information dialog box.

The dialog box contains two options:

• Click the first option button to open the file and the resource pool.

• Click the second option button to open only the file and not the resource pool. If you make changes to resource information while working with the file, Project will not be able to update the resource pool with these changes.

NOTE   *When you select the first option button, Project opens the resource pool as read-only so that other users can still work with other Project files that use the resource pool.*

Updating a Resource Pool

To update the resource pool if you make changes to resource information in the file, choose the Tools menu's Resources command and choose the submenu's Update Resource Pool command. If you forget to do this and attempt to close the project file, Project prompts you to update the resource pool.

Unlinking a Resource Pool

To stop sharing resources in a project, open the project, choose the Tools menu's Resources command, and choose the submenu's Share Resources command. Then click the Use Own Resources option button, and click OK.

To unlink a resource pool from multiple projects, take the following actions:

1. Open the resource pool file.

Open this file directly, in read-write mode.

2. Choose the Tools menu's Resources command, and choose the submenu's Share Resources command.

Project displays the Share Resources dialog box, as shown in Figure 4-25.

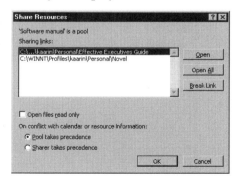

Figure 4-25   The Share Resources dialog box.

3. Select the projects you want to unlink from the resource pool.

The Sharing Links box lists all projects using resources from the resource pool. Select the projects you want to unlink from the resource pool.

4. Click the Break Link button.

5. Click OK.

Summary

After you've scheduled your project tasks and assigned resources to these tasks, you've accomplished the two major planning steps related to organizing a project. You're now ready to look over your work, as described in "Step 5: Review Project Organization."

Step 5

REVIEW PROJECT ORGANIZATION

Tasks Required to Complete the Step

- Outlining your project
- Changing the timescale
- Using filters
- Sorting tasks and resources
- Looking at your project in various views

Now that you've created the basic structure of your project and assigned resources to the various tasks, you'll want to take a good look at it before passing it around to your stakeholders—those people and groups that will either be involved in the project or affected by it. With Microsoft Project 2000, you can look at the organization of your project in myriad ways, each designed to focus on a particular aspect. With a simple project, you can often get most of the information you need from the Gantt Chart view. As your projects become more complex, however, you'll want to know how to manipulate them so that you can identify and scrutinize areas that are sure to produce surprises when you least expect them.

Outlining Your Project

You may have noticed in previous steps that one of the first tasks involved in a book-publishing project is creating an outline. Outlining is essential when you're preparing a document of almost anything more than a few paragraphs, as you probably remember from your high-school language arts classes. An outline provides the structure for organizing your thoughts and presenting them in a coherent manner.

An outline is equally important in project management for the same reason: it provides an ordered structure for the tasks in a project. Using an outline, you can group tasks and summarize their associated duration, cost, and resources.

Step 3 looked briefly at how you add summary tasks to a project, thus creating a simple outline. This step looks at this process in more detail and shows you how to use an outline to manage your project more effectively.

Using Summary Tasks

A *summary task* is a task in a project outline that has subordinate tasks, or *subtasks*. You can create an outline in two ways:

- From the top down, by identifying summary tasks
- From the bottom up, by listing all the subtasks

For example, if you're planning an off-site retreat or seminar for your department managers, you might have the following summary tasks:

1. Schedule a time.
2. Find and reserve a place.
3. Organize the agenda.
4. Determine the meal plan.

You can then break out the subtasks that each of these summary tasks involves. The first summary task might involve the following subtasks:

1. Check company schedule.
2. Check personal calendar.
3. Check managers' schedules.

Figure 5-1 shows how this summary task and its subtasks look in Project. If you need to refresh your memory about the actions required to enter summary tasks and subtasks, take a look back at Step 3.

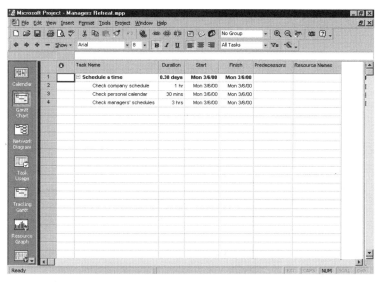

Figure 5-1   A summary task and its subtasks.

Sometimes, however, it's more useful to start with the subtasks and then insert summary tasks. In other words, work from the bottom up. Step 3 used this approach to enter the to-do list and then insert summary tasks.

You often need to do this when you're reviewing the organization of your project. For example, you may discover that a subtask involves sub-subtasks and really should be a summary task. As you recall, you define summary tasks by entering a task and then indenting the subtasks.

Using the Outlining Tools

Regardless of whether you choose the top-down or bottom-up approach to outlining, you use the outlining tools on the Formatting toolbar, as shown in Figure 5-2, to promote and demote tasks.

Figure 5-2   The outlining tools on the Formatting toolbar.

Click the Show button on the Formatting toolbar to display more or fewer levels of your outline. For example, if your outline has three levels, clicking Show and then clicking Outline Level 3 or All Subtasks displays all three levels. Clicking Show and then clicking Outline Level 2 displays only the first two levels and hides Level 3. Figure 5-3 shows a project that has four outline levels, and all are displayed. Figure 5-4 shows the same project with only two outline levels displayed.

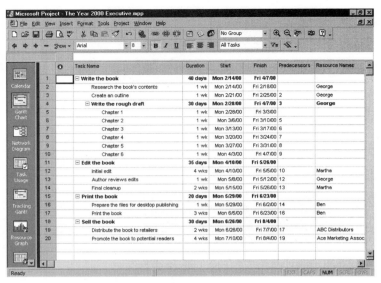

Figure 5-3   A project that has three outline levels.

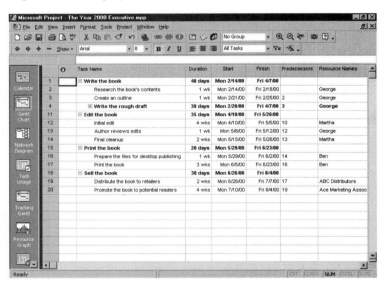

Figure 5-4   A project that has three outline levels, of which only two are displayed.

NOTE   *In Project, you can have as many as nine outline levels. That is, a summary task can have a maximum of eight levels of subtasks.*

Promoting and Demoting Tasks

To promote a task, you simply select it and click the Outdent toolbar button. It does not become a summary task, though, until you either insert subtasks or demote subsequent tasks. To demote a task, you select it and click the Indent toolbar button. When you demote a task or a group of tasks, you see the following changes:

- The task immediately preceding becomes a summary task and is in boldface.

- The selected tasks are indented to the right.

- A summary bar appears in the Gantt chart, as Figure 5-5 shows.

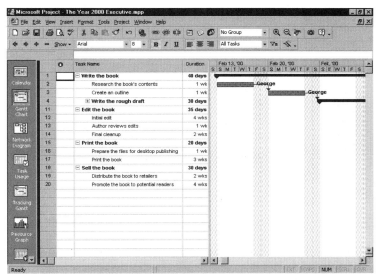

Figure 5-5   A Gantt chart with a summary bar.

Editing or Deleting Summary Tasks

As you're reviewing the organization of your project, you may well find that you want to change the wording of a summary task, for example, to more accurately reflect the grouping, and you may also want to delete a summary task. To change a summary task, simply select it and edit its contents in the Entry bar. (The Entry bar is the white space just below the Formatting toolbar.)

Deleting a summary task is a bit trickier than it might seem. The problem is that whenever you delete a summary task, you also delete its associated subtasks, and that isn't necessarily what you always want to do. To see how this works, take the following actions:

1. **Select a summary task in your project.**

   To select a task, simply click it.

2. **Press the Delete key.**

   You'll now see the Planning Wizard dialog box, as shown in Figure 5-6. The Planning Wizard warns you that deleting a summary task also deletes its subtasks and gives you the opportunity to change your mind.

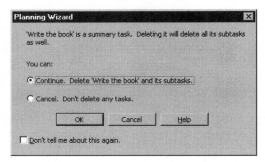

Figure 5-6   The Planning Wizard dialog box.

3. **If you want to delete both the summary task and its subtasks, click OK.**

   If you don't want to delete both kinds of tasks, click Cancel, and then click OK.

If you don't see the Planning Wizard dialog box, take the following actions:

1. **Choose the Tools menu's Options command.**

   Project displays the Options dialog box.

2. **Click the General tab.**

   Project displays the General tab of the Options dialog box, shown in Figure 5-7.

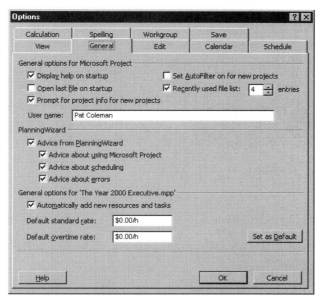

Figure 5-7   The General tab of the Options dialog box.

3. Select the Advice From PlanningWizard check box and all its subordinate check boxes.

4. Click OK.

This applies your changes and closes the Options dialog box.

TIP   *It's a good idea to leave all the wizards enabled until you become familiar with the way Project works. When they start to annoy you, you can clear the check boxes on the General tab of the Options dialog box to disable them.*

But you still need to know how to delete a summary task without deleting its subtasks, right? To do this, take the following actions:

1. Select the subtasks, and then click the Outdent toolbar button.

This promotes the subtasks to the same level as the summary task.

2. Select the summary task, and press the Delete key.

Moving Tasks and Summary Tasks

In the process of reviewing the organization of a project, you will very likely come across a task or a summary task that needs to be moved. For example, in the off-site seminar plan mentioned earlier in this step, suppose you want the event to take place at the Executive Plaza Resort, and you've found out that its conference rooms are booked except for one week this quarter and one week the next quarter. Because the date will now be determined by the availability of the place, you need to switch steps 1 and 2.

To switch tasks 1 and 2, take the following actions:

1. **Select task 2.**

   Click the gray number 2 box at the left end of the task to select the entire row.

2. **Hold down the left mouse button, and drag the cursor up until it rests on the line above task 1.**

   As you drag, you'll see a gray line appear.

3. **Release the mouse button.**

   Task 1 and task 2 are now switched. Notice that the durations, resources, and costs travel with the task when it is moved.

To move a group of tasks, take the following actions:

1. **Select the first task in the group.**

   Click the gray box at the left end of the task to select it.

2. **Press and hold down the Shift key, and select the number of the last task in the group.**

   This selects all the tasks in between as well.

3. **Release the mouse button and the Shift key.**

4. **Click the group that you just selected, and drag until you reach the line above the row where you want to relocate the tasks.**

   As you drag, a gray line appears.

5. **Release the mouse button.**

   This drops the group of tasks in the new location.

You move summary tasks in the same way that you move any other task. Remember, however, that all of a summary task's subtasks move right along with it, as well as all associated durations, resources, and costs. Another point to be aware of when moving summary tasks is that if you move a summary task into an existing summary group, the summary task you move becomes a subtask of that group. In addition, the subtasks of the summary task that you move then become sub-subtasks.

TIP   *Don't forget about the Undo toolbar button when you're moving tasks around. If you move a task to the wrong place, simply click Undo to restore it to its original location.*

Collapsing and Expanding Tasks

Another helpful way to look at your project, especially if it is long and complicated, is to collapse tasks. To hide an individual summary task's subtasks, click the minus sign next to the summary task. To then display the subtasks, click the plus sign. To display only the summary tasks in your project, take the following actions:

1. **Select the entire project by clicking the Select All button.**

   This button is the cell above the first ID number. The ID numbers are in the leftmost column of the Gantt table.

2. **Click the Hide Subtasks button on the Formatting toolbar.**

   Project collapses to the topmost summary task. So if you have a single summary task for the entire project, Project collapses the entire project. Click Show Subtasks to show the next level of summary tasks. Click Show Subtasks as many times as necessary to display all subtasks in the project.

Adding Outline Symbols and Numbers

By default, Project inserts plus and minus signs next to summary tasks. You can remove them if you want, and you can also number your outline using the options on the View tab of the Options dialog box. To do so, take the following actions:

1. **Choose the Tools menu's Options command.**

   Project displays the Options dialog box.

2. **Click the View tab.**

   Figure 5-8 shows this tab.

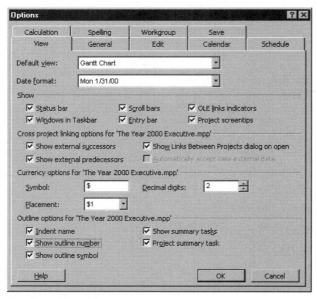

Figure 5-8   The View tab on the Options dialog box.

3. Select the Show Outline Number check box.

To hide the plus and minus signs, clear the Show Outline Symbol check box as well.

4. Click OK.

Table 5-1 lists and describes all the outlining options on the View tab.

NOTE   *Project uses the outlining structure that conforms to the WBS (Work Breakdown Structure) project management system, which organizes tasks to facilitate detailed reporting and tracking of costs.*

OPTION	WHAT IT DOES
Indent Name	Indents each level of subtask to the right. Clear this check box if you want to align, rather than indent, all subtasks.
Show Outline Number	Displays a number in front of all summary tasks and subtasks. Clear this check box if you don't want to use outline numbering.
Show Outline Symbol	Displays a plus/minus sign in front of each summary task. Clear this check box if you don't want to display these symbols.

OPTION	WHAT IT DOES
Show Summary Tasks	Displays summary tasks. Clear this check box if you don't want to display summary tasks.
Project Summary Task	Displays the name of your project in row 0 of the Gantt table. Clear this check box if you don't want to display the project name.

Table 5-1   Outlining options in Project.

Depending on how you plan to use the information you're storing in your project, outlining can come in handy. Figure 5-9 shows a project that uses outline numbering and displays the summary project task in row 0.

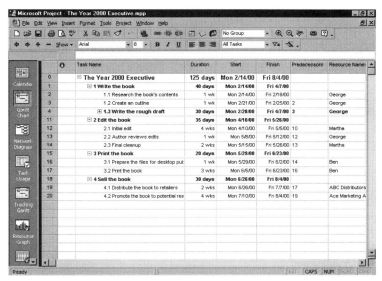

Figure 5-9   A project that uses outline numbering, indents tasks, and includes the project summary task or name of the project.

Changing the Timescale

By default, the timescale on the Gantt chart displays days on the minor scale and weeks on the major scale, as shown in Figure 5-10. You can easily change the timescale to display more or less detail by clicking the Zoom In and Zoom Out toolbar buttons. You can zoom out all the way to half-year intervals, and you can zoom in all the way to quarter-hour intervals.

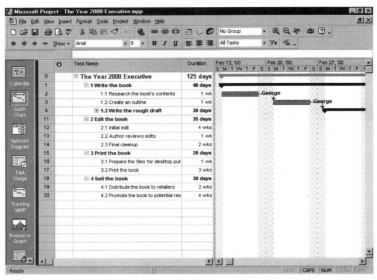

Figure 5-10　By default, the Gantt chart timescale displays days and weeks.

Depending on the complexity and scope of your project, you may find it helpful to zoom out and take a look at the big picture—either on the screen or in print. (Step 6 discusses printing.) Figure 5-11 shows the same project as in Figure 5-10, but the timescale has been zoomed out to display the months of the year, rather than the days and weeks.

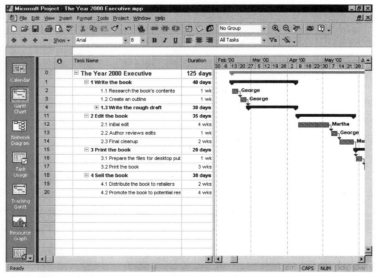

Figure 5-11　The timescale is zoomed out to show months and years.

Using Filters

Thus far, you've seen a number of ways that you can view and manipulate the information in a project, but this book has only just begun to introduce you to the myriad features at your disposal once the to-do list in your head is in electronic form. This section looks at *filters*. Don't be put off by the "techie" sound of this term. A filter is simply a device you can use to segregate and display only specific information. For example, suppose you want to see only the tasks that one person will perform on the current project or only tasks that are not yet complete. To get this information, you use a filter.

Project has two kinds of filters:

- Standard filters that are predefined in Project
- Filters that you create

Each type serves a particular purpose, and this section gives you some tips for when you might want to use each.

The default filter is All Tasks. You can always tell which filter is active by looking at the Filter box, as shown in Figure 5-12. To return to the default filter at any time, press F3.

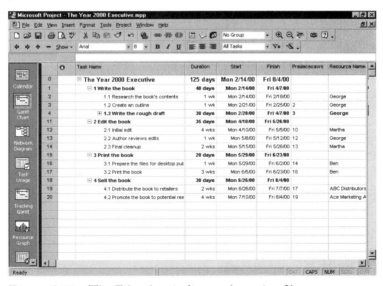

Figure 5-12 The Filter box indicates the active filter.

Standard Filters

Project provides 56 standard filters, and they are of two types:

- Task filters
- Resource filters

As their names suggest, task filters let you segregate information about tasks, such as which are complete, which are not yet started, which are associated with overtime, and so on. Task filters are available when using views that are primarily task-based, such as the Calendar and Gantt chart views. Resource filters let you segregate information about resources, such as which are overallocated, which are slipping behind in completing their tasks, and so on. Resource filters are available when using views that are primarily resource-based, such as the Resource Graph and Resource Sheet views. Table 5-2 lists and describes the task filters, and Table 5-3 lists and describes the resource filters.

FILTER	WHAT IT SHOWS
All Tasks	All tasks in the project.
Completed Tasks	All finished tasks.
Confirmed	The tasks that resources have agreed to accept.
Cost Greater Than	The tasks that will cost more than the amount you designate.
Cost Overbudget	Tasks that will cost more than the baseline amount. This is a calculated filter.
Created After	All tasks that were created after a date you specify. This is an interactive filter.
Critical	All tasks on the critical path.
Date Range	All tasks that start or finish between two dates that you specify. This is an interactive filter.
In Progress Tasks	All tasks that have begun but are not finished.
Incomplete Tasks	All unfinished tasks.
Late/Overbudget Tasks Assigned To	Tasks associated with the resource you specify that exceed the budget or that will finish after the baseline finish date.
Linked Fields	Tasks that are linked to values in another program, such as a worksheet in Microsoft Excel.
Milestones	All tasks that are milestones.
Resource Group	Tasks associated with the resources of the group you specify. This is an interactive filter.

FILTER	WHAT IT SHOWS
Should Start By	All tasks that should have started by a date you specify but have not done so. This is an interactive filter.
Should Start/Finish By	Tasks that haven't started and finished within a date range that you specify. This is an interactive filter.
Slipped/Late Progress	Tasks that are behind the scheduled finish date or that are not moving along on schedule.
Slipping Tasks	All tasks that are running behind schedule.
Summary Tasks	All tasks that have subtasks.
Task Range	All tasks that have ID numbers within a range you specify. This is an interactive filter.
Tasks with Attachments	All tasks that have an attached object or a note.
Tasks with a Task Calendar Assigned	Tasks that have objects and a calendar associated with them.
Tasks with Deadlines	Tasks for which you set a deadline.
Tasks with Estimated Durations	Tasks for which you specified that the duration was an estimate.
Tasks with Fixed Dates	All tasks that do not have the As Soon As Possible constraint or that have an actual start date.
Tasks/Assignments with Overtime	Tasks for which resources are working overtime.
Top Level Tasks	The highest-level tasks. Use this filter if your project has summary tasks within summary tasks.
Unconfirmed	Tasks for which you have requested resources and at least one resource has declined to accept.
Unstarted Tasks	Tasks not yet begun.
Update Needed	Revised tasks that need to be sent for update or confirmation.
Using Resource in Date Range	All tasks assigned to a resource that you specify that start and finish within dates you specify. This is an interactive filter.
Using Resource	All tasks that use the resource you specify. This is an interactive filter.
Work Overbudget	All tasks with scheduled work that is more than their baseline work. This is a calculated filter.

Table 5-2 The task filters.

RESOURCE	WHAT IT SHOWS
All Resources	All the resources in a project.
Confirmed Assignments	All assignments that have been accepted by their resources. You can use this filter only in the Resource Usage view.
Cost Greater Than	All resources that will cost more than the amount you specify. This is an interactive filter.
Cost Overbudget	All resources that have a scheduled cost that is more than their baseline cost. This is a calculated filter.
Date Range	All tasks and resources that start or finish within a date range that you supply. This is an interactive filter.
Group	All resources that belong to a group you specify. This is an interactive filter.
In Progress Assignments	Assignments that are started but that are not finished. You can use this filter only in Resource Usage view.
Linked Fields	Resources to which text from another application is linked, such as Microsoft Word.
Overallocated Resources	Resources that you have assigned more work than is possible in the allotted time.
Resource Range	All resources within a range of ID numbers that you specify. This is an interactive filter.
Resources – Material	All non-human resources, such as computers, paper, calculators, and so on.
Resources with Attachments	Resource to which objects or notes are attached.
Resources/Assignments with Overtime	Resources or assignments that are working overtime.
Resources – Work	Resources such as people or equipment.
Should Start By	All tasks and resources that should start by a date that you specify but have not done so. This is an interactive filter.
Should Start/Finish By	Tasks that should have started and finished within a date range you specify. This is an interactive filter.
Slipped/Late Progress	Resources whose tasks have not been finished by their baseline finish date or that are moving along on schedule.

RESOURCE	WHAT IT SHOWS
Slipping Assignments	Resources whose tasks are not moving along according to their baseline plan and are not yet completed.
Unconfirmed Assignments	Assignments that have not been accepted by their resources.
Unstarted Assignments	Assignments that have not yet begun.
Work Complete	Resources that have finished all their assigned tasks.
Work Incomplete	Resources that have scheduled work less than their baseline work. This is a calculated filter.
Work Overbudget	Resources that have scheduled work that is more than their baseline work. This is a calculated filter.

Table 5-3   The resource filters.

In most views, you can access all the standard filters, as well as filters you create, by using the following tools:

- The Filtered For command
- The Filter box
- The More Filters command
- The AutoFilter command

Each tool gives you a distinct view of the filtered information.

As this section details the different ways that you can apply filters, you'll begin to notice that you can get the same information in various ways. For example, you can display all the tasks that one person is responsible for by using an AutoFilter or by using an interactive filter. Which method you use depends partly on the view and partly on your personal preference.

Using a filter to segregate information does just that. It does not change or remove any of the information in your project. And don't forget: to return to the default view (All Tasks) at any time, simply press F3.

NOTE   *When you apply one filter and then apply a second filter, the second filter applies to the entire project, not just to the information that was displayed when you ran the first filter.*

Access Filters with the Filtered For Command

NOTE *The following section discusses task filters. The same techniques apply to resource filters.*

You use the Filtered For command to access ten commonly used filters, as well as the More Filters command:

- All Tasks
- Completed Tasks
- Critical
- Date Range
- Incomplete Tasks
- Milestones
- Summary Tasks
- Task Range
- Tasks with Estimated Durations
- Using Resource

To use the Filtered For command to display all completed tasks, choose the Project menu's Filtered For: command and the submenu's Completed Tasks command. Figure 5-13 shows only the completed tasks for the book-publishing project. This type of filtered view is called an *isolated filter view*.

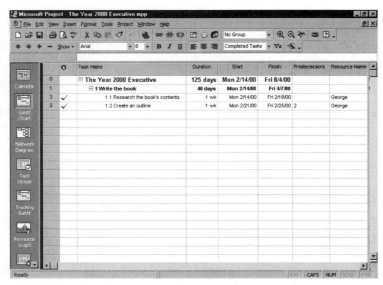

Figure 5-13   The book-publishing project, filtered for completed tasks.

Instead of displaying only the completed tasks, you can also display the entire project and display completed tasks in a different color. This type of filtered view is called a *highlighted filter view*. To do this, take the following actions:

1. **Hold down the Shift key.**

2. **Choose the Project menu's Filtered For: command and the submenu's Completed Tasks command.**

   Project displays the completed tasks in a different color.

Access Filters with the Filter Box

As mentioned earlier, you can always tell which filter is active by looking at the Filter box, but you can also use the Filter box to select and apply a filter. Click the drop-down arrow, and then scroll down through the list to see the available filters. The Filter box displays the standard filters and the filters you create. You can't use the Filter box to select a highlighted filter though. (Later in this section, we'll look at how to create your own filters.)

Access Filters with the More Filters Command

You can use the More Filters command to apply other filters, but its real purpose is to allow you to select, edit, create, format, and organize filters. Earlier we looked at how to display filtered tasks in a color that is different from the color of the other tasks. By default, that color is blue, but you can change it to another color using the More Filters dialog box and the Text Styles dialog box. To do this, take the following actions:

1. **Choose the Project menu's Filtered For: command, and then select the submenu's More Filters command.**

   Project displays the More Filters dialog box, as shown in Figure 5-14.

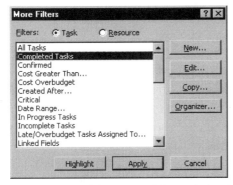

Figure 5-14   The More Filters dialog box.

2. **Select a filter, and then click the Highlight button.**

   The filtered tasks you selected now appear in blue.

3. **Choose the Format menu's Text Styles command.**

   Project displays the Text Styles dialog box, as shown in Figure 5-15.

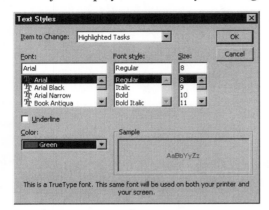

Figure 5-15 The Text Styles dialog box.

4. **Select Highlighted Tasks from the Item To Change drop-down list box.**

TIP *This list isn't in alphabetic order, and you'll need to scroll down to about the middle to find Highlighted Tasks.*

5. **Select a color from the Color drop-down list box, and then click OK.**

   What was formerly blue is now displayed in the color you selected. You can also use the Text Styles dialog box to change the font, the font size, and emphasis (such as bold or italic).

You can, of course, use the More Filters box to simply apply a filter. To do so, select the filter and then click the Apply button. A later section looks at how to use the More Filters dialog box to create your own filter.

Using AutoFilters

An AutoFilter applies to a single column in a Gantt table. For example, you can choose the Today AutoFilter in the Finish column to display only the tasks in your project that will be completed today. By default, AutoFilters are not enabled; to turn them on, click the AutoFilter button on the Formatting toolbar. You'll then see a drop-down arrow on the right of each column heading.

Figure 5-16 shows AutoFilters turned on and the drop-down menu that appears when you click the Resource Names AutoFilter.

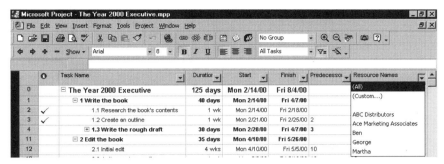

Figure 5-16 Click the name George to display only the tasks that George will perform in this project.

To get an idea of what filters are available with AutoFilter, take a moment to click the drop-down arrow and check out the menu that appears with each column in the Gantt table.

NOTE *You cannot apply AutoFilters in the Calendar, Resource Graph, Network Diagram, or Form views.*

An important feature of AutoFilter is the Custom command, which might sound advanced but is really simple to use. Let's use it to filter out a start date. To do this, take the following actions:

1. Click the down arrow in the Start column of the Gantt table, and select Custom.

Project displays the Custom AutoFilter dialog box, as shown in Figure 5-17.

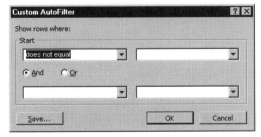

Figure 5-17 The Custom AutoFilter dialog box.

2. Select Does Not Equal from the Start drop-down list box.

The items in this drop-down list are called *comparison operators*.

3. In the drop-down box to the right, select a date.

4. Click OK.

Now all tasks associated with the start date you selected are filtered out.

Using Interactive Filters

If you perused Tables 5-2 and 5-3 earlier in this step, you noticed that some filters are described as "interactive." An interactive filter requires that you specify some information, such as the name of a resource or a date range. If a filter is interactive, its name in the Filtered For: All Tasks submenu is followed by an ellipsis (...). As is the case in all Microsoft Windows programs, an ellipsis indicates that clicking the item opens a dialog box.

When you're using an interactive filter, you use its dialog box to enter information. To see how this works, let's filter for a task range. To do this, take the following actions:

1. **Choose the Project menu's Filtered For: command, and choose the submenu's Task Range command.**

   Project displays the Task Range dialog box, as shown in Figure 5-18.

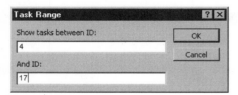

Figure 5-18   The Task Range dialog box.

2. **Specify the ID range of the tasks you want to display.**

   In the Show Tasks Between ID text box, enter the first ID of the range of tasks you want to display. In the And ID text box, enter the last ID of the range of tasks you want to display.

3. **Click OK.**

   Now you'll see only tasks that fall within the range of ID numbers you specified.

TIP   *If you want to highlight the task range rather than displaying it in isolated filter view, press and hold down the Shift key while taking action 1.*

Creating a Filter

With all the predefined filters at your fingertips, you might find it difficult to imagine why you would ever need to define a custom filter. The time will come, however, and then you can turn back to this section of the book for details.

You can create a new filter from scratch, or you can edit an existing filter to accommodate your needs. Let's start with the latter.

Editing an Existing Filter

To create a new filter from an existing one, take the following actions:

1. **Choose the Project menu's Filtered For: command, and then choose the submenu's More Filters command.**

   Project displays the More Filters dialog box.

2. **If necessary, select the Task option, and then select a filter from the list.**

3. **Click Copy.**

   Project displays the Filter Definition dialog box, as shown in Figure 5-19.

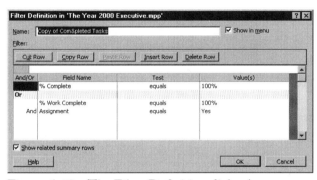

Figure 5-19 The Filter Definition dialog box.

4. **Type a name for your new filter in the Name box.**

   Select the Show In Menu check box so that your new filter will appear in the Filtered For submenu. If necessary, select the Field Name and change it.

5. **Specify the criteria a task must meet for Project to display or highlight it.**

   Select the contents in the Test column, and click the down arrow to select a comparison operator. Select the contents in the Value(s) column, and click the down arrow to select a value.

6. **Click OK.**

   The name of your new filter appears in the More Filters dialog box. To apply it, click Apply.

Creating a New Filter

To create a new filter, take the following actions:

1. **Choose the Project menu's Filtered For: command, and then choose the submenu's More Filters command.**

   Project displays the More Filters dialog box.

2. Click New.

Project displays the Filter Definition dialog box, empty and ready for you to use it to create a new filter, as shown in Figure 5-20.

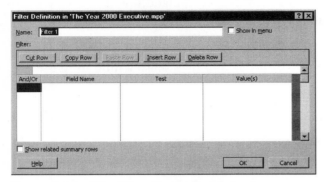

Figure 5-20   The Filter Definition dialog box.

3. Name the new filter.

Enter a name for your new filter in the Name box.

4. Select the Show In Menu check box.

When you select this option, Project lists the name of your new filter in the Filtered For menu.

5. Specify the criteria a task must meet for Project to display or highlight it.

Select the Field Name box, and then click the down arrow to select a field from the list. Select the Test box, and then click the down arrow to select a comparison operator from the list. Select the Value(s) box, and then click the down arrow to select a value from the list.

6. Click OK.

Sorting Tasks and Resources

Yet another way to look at the information in your project is to sort it. For example, you could arrange tasks or resources in alphabetic order instead of ID number order. You may remember that when you apply a filter to a project and then apply another filter, the second filter works on the entire project, not on the display that resulted from the first filter.

When you're sorting in Project, however, you need to be aware that the sort will apply to the current view. If you filter on Summary Tasks, for example, and then run a sort, the sort applies only to Summary Tasks, which are displayed in the current view.

To see how sorting works, let's sort on Resource Names. If you have a large, complicated project, you might very well want to do this and then print your Gantt table so that all the people involved in the project can see at a glance the tasks for which they are responsible and the part of the schedule that involves them. Take the following actions:

1. **Switch to the Task Sheet view.**

    Choose the View menu's More Views command to open the More Views dialog box, as shown in Figure 5-21, select Task Sheet, and then click the Apply button.

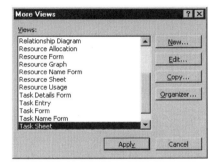

Figure 5-21   The More Views dialog box.

2. **Choose the Project menu's Sort command, and then choose the submenu's Sort By command.**

    Project displays the Sort dialog box, as shown in Figure 5-22.

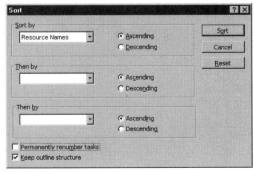

Figure 5-22   The Sort dialog box.

3. **In the Sort By box, click the down arrow and select Resource Names from the list.**

4. **Make sure that the Permanently Renumber Tasks check box is cleared.**

   If you allow Project to permanently renumber tasks when sorting, you can get some unexpected and unwanted results that can damage your task relationships. Of course, if this happens, you can always click the Undo toolbar button and sort again after you clear this check box.

5. **Leave the Keep Outline Structure check box selected.**

   If you clear the Permanently Renumber Tasks check box and leave the Keep Outline Structure check box selected, Project will not reassign ID numbers, and, in addition, all subtasks will stay with their summary tasks.

6. **Click the Sort button.**

Figure 5-23 shows a small project sorted by Resource Names.

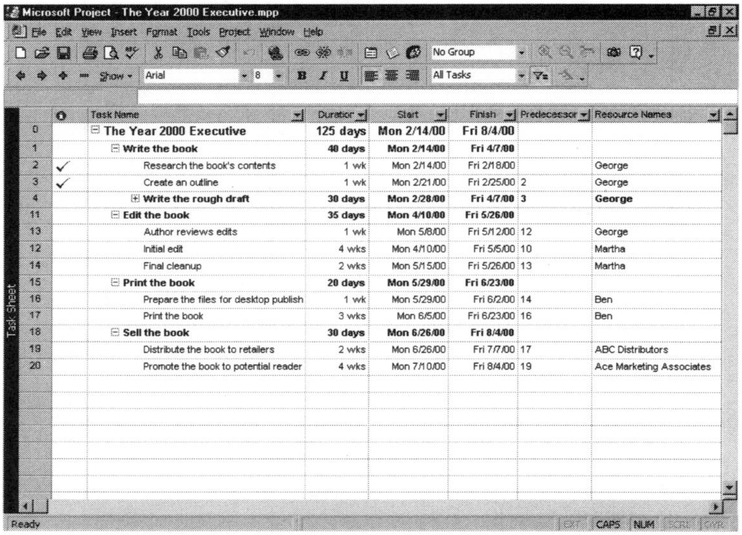

Figure 5-23   A book-publishing project sorted by Resource Names.

Looking at Your Project in Various Views

In Project, a view is simply a way to display the information in a project. You can look at your project in various views to focus on its different aspects. The default view, which you've seen many times in this book, is the Gantt Chart view, which is actually a table and a bar chart. In this view, you enter task information in the pane on the left, and the chart in the pane on the right displays a graphical representation of that information.

If, however, you want to zero in on a particular aspect of your project, you can display the information in a different view. For example, if you want to check out resource allocations, you'll probably want to display your project in Resource Graph view, as demonstrated in Step 4.

Understanding the Types of Views

In Project, you can display information in three types of views:

- Chart or graph, which presents information as pictures
- Sheet, which presents information as it might appear in a table or a worksheet
- Form, which presents information about a single task as it might appear on a paper form

Views can also be categorized according to whether they contain information about tasks or resources. For example, the Gantt Chart view is a task view. In Step 4, you looked at three types of resource views:

- Resource Sheet
- Resource Graph
- Resource Usage

Table 5-4 lists the available views in Project and describes the circumstance in which each is used. The following sections look at some of these views in detail, and discuss how to create a new view. To display one of the most commonly used views, click its button on the View Bar. To display any of the other default views, take the following actions:

1. Click the More Views button on the View Bar.

Project displays the More Views dialog box, as shown in Figure 5-24.

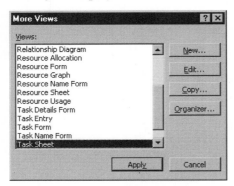

Figure 5-24 The More Views dialog box.

2. Select a view from the Views list, and then click the Apply button.

VIEW	WHAT IT SHOWS	USE IT TO
Bar Rollup	A list of summary tasks and labels for all subtasks.	Display all tasks concisely labeled on summary task bars.
Calendar	A one-month calendar of tasks and durations.	Display the scheduled tasks for a range of weeks.
Detail Gantt	Tasks, related information, and a chart.	Determine how much a task can slip without affecting other tasks.
Gantt Chart	Entry table and a chart.	Enter and schedule tasks.
Leveling Gantt	Task list, tasks delays and slack, and a bar chart that shows the effects before and after leveling.	Check for task delay.
Milestone Date Rollup	Summary tasks and labels for all subtasks.	See tasks concisely labeled and milestone marks and dates on summary task bars.
Milestone Rollup	Summary tasks that contain labels for all subtasks.	See tasks concisely labeled and milestone marks on summary task bars.
Network Diagram	A graphical representation of all tasks and task dependencies.	Create and adjust your schedule in flowchart format.
Relationship Diagram	A graphical representation of the predecessors and successors or a single task.	Focus on the dependencies of a single task.

VIEW	WHAT IT SHOWS	USE IT TO
Resource Allocation	The Resource Usage view in the top pane and the Leveling Gantt view in the bottom pane.	Resolve overallocations of resources.
Resource Form	A paperlike form.	Enter and edit information about a single resource.
Resource Graph	A visual representation of resource allocation, cost, or overtime.	Display information about a single resource or a group of resources.
Resource Name Form	A paperlike form.	Enter and edit resource information.
Resource Sheet	A table of resources and related information.	Enter and edit resource information in a worksheet format.
Resource Usage	A list of resource allocation, cost, or work information over time.	Display cost or work allocation information for each resource and set resource contours.
Task Details Form	A paperlike form.	Review and edit tracking and scheduling information for a single task.
Task Entry	The Gantt Chart view in the top pane and the Task Form view in the bottom pane.	Add, edit, and review information about the task selected in the Gantt chart.
Task Form	A paperlike form.	Enter and edit information about a single task.
Task Name Form	A paperlike form.	Enter and edit the task name and other information.
Task Sheet	A table of tasks and related information.	Enter and schedule tasks in a worksheet format.
Task Usage	A task list that shows resources grouped under each task.	Determine which resources are assigned to which tasks and set resource work contours.
Tracking Gantt	A task list and related information, and a chart showing baseline and Gantt bars.	Compare the baseline schedule with the actual schedule.

Table 5-4   Available views in Project.

Before delving into some of the views on the View Bar as well as some of the other available views, we need to look at the different ways you can view tables that are contained in views. Not all views contain tables, but all tables are contained in views. One that you know very well by now is the entry table in the Gantt Chart view. If you open the Gantt Chart view and right-click the Select All button, you'll see a list of table views, as shown in Figure 5-25. You can select one of these table views, or you can click the More Tables button to open the More Tables dialog box, as shown in Figure 5-26. The More Tables dialog box contains a list of all the available table views in Project. Click a table, and then click the Apply button to open a table in that view.

Figure 5-25   Click the Select All button to display a list of table views.

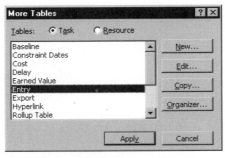

Figure 5-26   The More Tables dialog box displays a list of all the available table views.

The Views on the View Bar

Earlier parts of this book described some of the views on the View Bar. This section takes a look at those not discussed earlier. Let's begin with the Calendar view.

TIP   *If the View Bar isn't visible, choose the View menu's View Bar command.*

Calendar View

Click the Calendar icon on the View Bar to display a screen similar to that shown in Figure 5-27.

NOTE   *The remainder of this step looks at how the book-publishing project appears in various views. Although some views may not be as practical as others, you'll get an idea of how different views can be effective when you're reviewing project organization.*

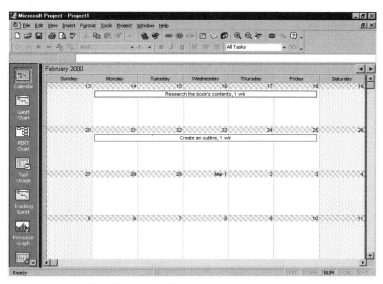

Figure 5-27   The book-publishing project in Calendar view.

Before the invention of Project or any other electronic project-management tool (or even personal computers, for that matter), people used an enormous paper version of this view to track projects. People would often put a calendar and schedule on a roll of butcher paper and then tack it to the wall—all around the room. Maybe that's why this view looks so familiar?

In Project's Calendar view, the number of weeks you see when you first open Calendar view depends on the resolution of your monitor. At 800 by 600 resolution, the calendar displays four weeks, as you can see in Figure 5-27. To display more or fewer weeks, take the following actions:

1. **Right-click an empty area of the calendar, and choose the shortcut menu's Zoom command.**

   Project displays the Zoom dialog box, as shown in Figure 5-28.

Figure 5-28   Use the Zoom dialog box to change the number of weeks displayed in Calendar view.

2. **Select the number of weeks you want to display and the time period, and then click OK.**

To view the previous month, click the left-pointing arrow in the top-right corner of the view. To display the next month, click the right-pointing arrow. You can also look at subsequent or previous months by dragging the slider on the vertical scroll bar.

TIP   *Don't confuse the Calendar view with the project calendar that you use to tell Project how to handle events such as holidays and other nonworking time.*

To change the information about a single task in the calendar, right-click the task and choose the shortcut menu's Task Information command to open the Task Information dialog box.

NOTE   *You can, of course, print views, and the next step describes how to do so.*

Network Diagram View

If you're accustomed to working with flowcharts, you may find it effective to use the Network Diagram view. Figure 5-29 shows the book-publishing project open in Network Diagram view.

NOTE *If you had Project 98 on your computer and upgraded to Project 2000, the Network Diagram view may still be called the PERT Chart view.*

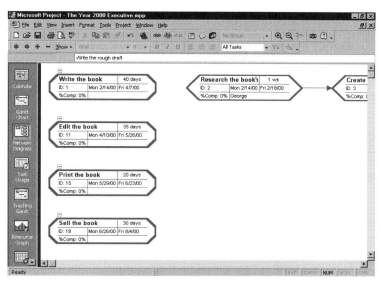

Figure 5-29 The book-publishing project open in Network Diagram view.

In this view, a box, or node, represents a task, and a line represents a dependency between tasks. A diagonal line through a task indicates that the task is in progress, and crossed diagonal lines indicate that a task is completed. To edit the information in a task box, double-click the box to open the Task Information dialog box.

If you want to adjust the position of boxes manually, choose the Format menu's Layout command to open the Layout dialog box, as shown in Figure 5-30. In this dialog box, you can also adjust the colors of the flowchart, specify whether to show summary tasks, adjust page breaks, and so on.

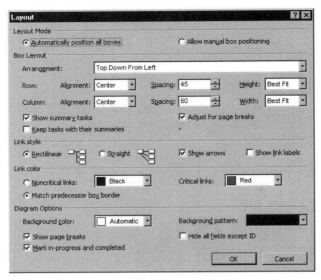

Figure 5-30 The Layout dialog box.

The Network Diagram view is the best view to use when you want to do the following:

- Link tasks and specify start and finish dates
- Display complete, in-progress, and not-yet-started tasks in graphical format
- Associate resources with specific tasks

NOTE   *Project 2000's Network Diagram view closely resembles the PERT Chart view from earlier versions of Project. You can accomplish many of the same tasks in Network Diagram view as you could with the PERT Chart view. Appendix A details how you work with Network Diagram view and perform what-if analysis.*

Task Usage View

You use this view when you want to focus on how much work each resource has performed on a task. Figure 5-31 shows the book-publishing project in Task Usage view. The table part of this view shows task information, and the chart portion shows resource information.

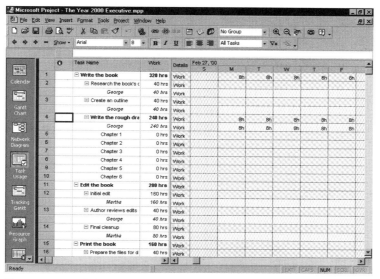

Figure 5-31   The book-publishing project in Task Usage view.

The Task Usage view is the best view to use when you want to do the following:

- Organize your resources by tasks
- Evaluate the work effort or the costs by task
- Compare the schedule with actual work performed
- Compare the planned costs with the actual costs

You can edit the entry table of this view in the same way that you edit the entry table in the Gantt Chart view.

Tracking Gantt View

This view can become one of your best friends when you're tracking the progress of your project. It's a visual representation of how your project stacks up when compared with the baseline. Figure 5-32 shows the book-publishing project in Tracking Gantt view.

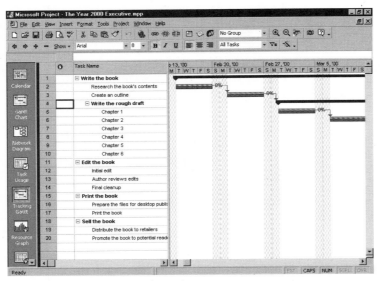

Figure 5-32   The book-publishing project in Tracking Gantt view.

Step 7 revisits this view and look at how you update your project to track actual work and costs.

Now that you're on speaking terms with the most commonly used views, let's take a look at some of the other available views and how you can use them to review the organization of your project.

More Views

As mentioned at the beginning of this section on views, you click More Views on the View Bar to open the More Views dialog box, which contains a list of all the views available in Project.

Let's start our tour of more views with the Detail Gantt view.

Detail Gantt View

You use this view to focus on slack and slippage. *Slack* is "extra time," that is, the days between the time one task ends and another starts. If you're like us, this is not something you often have to worry about when scheduling a project, but it's theoretically possible. Actually, good project management involves building in slack for the unexpected—illness, breakdown of equipment, and the like. *Slippage* may be a term you're all too familiar with. Slippage occurs when a task doesn't start on time or fails to progress according to schedule.

Figure 5-33 shows the book-publishing project in Detail Gantt view. As you can see, the only slack time for the writing portion of the schedule is the weekend. It's represented by a thin line that crosses from the end of Friday to the beginning of Monday.

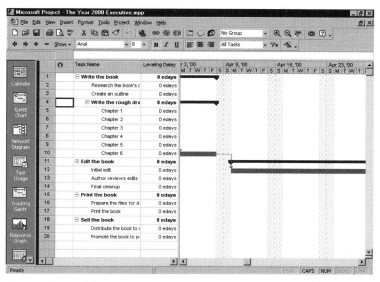

Figure 5-33   The book-publishing project in Detail Gantt view.

When you notice that a task is slipping, you'll probably want more detail, and so this is a good time to look at a combination view of the Detail Gantt and the Task Details form. The last section in this step, "Displaying a Combination of Views," does just this.

Leveling Gantt View

Step 4 discusses leveling resources, that is, resolving resource overallocation by adding resources, reducing durations, or eliminating constraints. You can view the effects of leveling resources in this view. The table portion of this view shows a list of tasks and information about delays. The chart portion shows a graphical representation of the tasks before and after leveling. Figure 5-34 shows the book-publishing project in Leveling Gantt view.

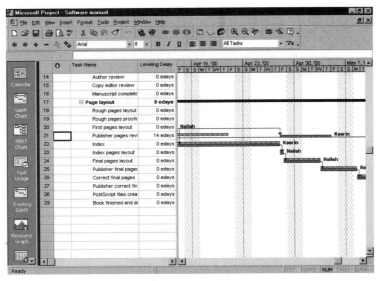

Figure 5-34 The book-publishing project in Leveling Gantt view.

To display more tasks on the timescale of the chart, click the Zoom Out toolbar button. To insert a task in the table, click the task above which you want to insert a new task, and then choose the Insert menu's New Task command.

Resource Form

This view displays information about a specific resource. First, select the name of a resource in any view, and then select the Resource Form view in the More Views dialog box. Figure 5-35 shows the Resource Form for George, the writer for the book-publishing project.

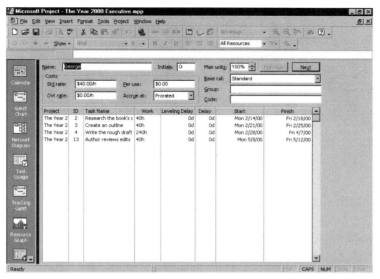

Figure 5-35 The Resource Form.

You can use this view to edit and enter information about the resource. To see other resources, click the Previous and Next buttons at the top right of this form. Unless you've sorted or filtered resources, they display in ID number order.

Resource Name Form View

This view is a stripped-down version of the Resource Form view. You can use it to enter and edit basic information about a resource. As you can do with the Resource Form, click the Previous or Next button to display this view for another resource. Figure 5-36 shows the Resource Name Form for George.

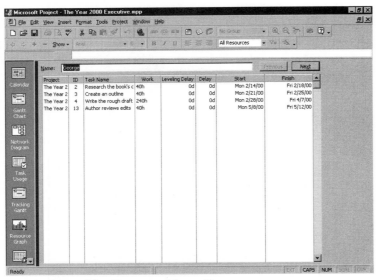

Figure 5-36   The Resource Name Form.

Task Details Form View

You use this view to display detailed information about a single task. First, select the task in any view, and then choose the Task Details view from the More Views dialog box. Figure 5-37 shows the Print The Book task from the book-publishing project in Task Details Form view. Click the Previous or Next button to display details about another task.

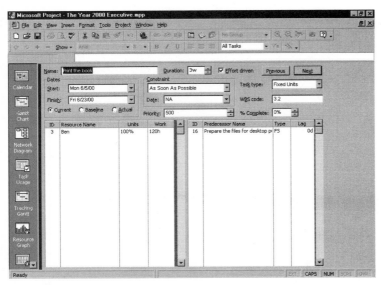

Figure 5-37   The Task Details Form.

The views you use when reviewing or working on any project depend, of course, on what you want to know. You'll probably find yourself most often using the views found on the View Bar, but take a little time to experiment with the other views available in the More Views dialog box so that you'll have an idea about what you might find helpful in a specific situation.

Now let's look at one more way you can view information in Project—a combination view.

Displaying a Combination of Views

As mentioned earlier in the discussion of the Detail Gantt view, you can display two views in a split window. For example, while displaying the Detail Gantt view, select a task, and choose the Window menu's Split command to display the Detail Gantt view in the top pane and a form view in the bottom pane. Figure 5-38 shows the book-publishing project in such a combination view.

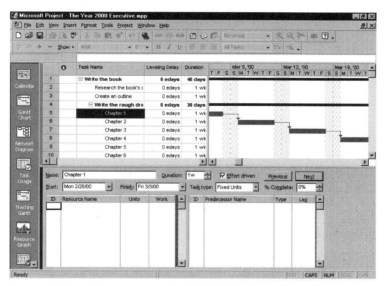

Figure 5-38   This combination view shows the Task Form view in the lower pane.

To change the view in the lower pane, click in the lower pane and choose a view from the View Bar.

Creating a New View

Although Project provides dozens of views that you can work with, the time may come that you need to create a new view. When you do so, you can include it on the View Bar or place it on the list of available views in the More Views dialog box. To create a new view, take the following actions:

1. **Open the More Views dialog box, and click New.**

   Project displays the Define New View dialog box, as shown in Figure 5-39.

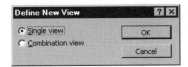

Figure 5-39   The Define New View dialog box.

2. **Click the Single View option button, and then click OK.**

   Project displays the View Definition dialog box, as shown in Figure 5-40.

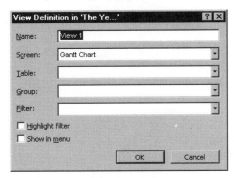

Figure 5-40   The View Definition dialog box.

3. **Name the new view.**

   Enter a name for your new view in the Name box.

4. **Select an available view on which to base your new view.**

   Select an existing view from the Screen drop-down list box.

5. **If the screen you select has a table, choose the table view from the Table drop-down list box.**

6. **If you want to specify a grouping, select it from the Group drop-down list box.**

7. **Optionally, specify a filter to apply to the view.**

   If you want to apply a filter other than All Tasks, select it from the Filter drop-down list box.

8. **If you want the information in your new view to display in the highlighted filter view, select the Highlight Filter check box.**

   Instead of omitting tasks that do not fit the filter criteria from the view, Project displays all tasks and colors those that fit the criteria.

9. **If you want the name of the new view to appear in the View Bar and on the View menu, select the Show In Menu check box.**

   Otherwise, the name of the new view will appear only in the list in the More Views dialog box.

10. **Click OK, and then click the Apply button.**

    Project saves the new view and opens the current project in the new view.

Summary

We once worked for a manager who started and ended every meeting with potential suppliers by saying that he wanted no surprises. As you well know, surprises aren't always a bad thing, but in the area of project management, surprises are almost always bad—unless your project finishes ahead of schedule and under budget.

The techniques talked about in this step are guaranteed to help you avoid bad surprises. Outlining your project, checking the schedule with various timescales, filtering and sorting tasks and resources, and taking a look at your project in various views provide good protection against surprises that can thwart your project if not throw it into a complete tailspin. You'll want to make these review processes part of your checklist before presenting your project to the stakeholders—the topic of Step 6.

Step 6

PRESENT PROJECT TO STAKEHOLDERS

Tasks Required to Complete the Step

- Printing views of your project
- Generating reports
- Exporting project information to other applications

As mentioned in previous steps, a stakeholder is any organization or individual that is involved in or affected by your project. Obviously, communicating with your stakeholders is an important aspect of your job as project manager. Initially, you want your stakeholders to understand the scope of the project and their individual responsibilities, which can include everything from participating in the project to having ultimate financial say-so about whether the project even gets off the ground.

Once your project is underway, you need to keep stakeholders informed about its progress—the schedule, the costs, the availability of resources, and so on. Upper management may require periodic reports at specified intervals and may even dictate the nature of those reports.

Depending on the technological sophistication of your organization, you may be able to distribute project news via a company intranet, over e-mail, or by means of the Internet. Appendix C explains what you need to know to do this.

This step describes printing the views discussed in Step 5, generating and printing reports based on the information you've collected, and exporting Microsoft Project information to other applications. Don't fret if this exporting business sounds too technical for you; it's really not difficult once you get the hang of it, and it's a very common practice.

Printing Views of Your Project

In Project, you can print views, and you can print reports. If you've printed when using other Microsoft Windows applications, the process and the dialog boxes will look familiar. Printing a view can be as simple as opening a view and clicking the Print toolbar button. The cost of this simplicity is that you don't have any control over how and exactly what is printed. Your view is printed with the predefined default settings, which often is not what you want.

Before delving into how you specify your own settings, let's take a look at the Print Preview feature, which, as you may know from other Windows applications, displays your document on the screen just as it will appear on the printed page.

Using Print Preview

You can access Print Preview in four ways:

- By clicking the Print Preview toolbar button
- By clicking the Preview button in the Print dialog box
- By choosing the File menu's Print Preview command
- By clicking the Print Preview button in the Page Setup dialog box

When you select Print Preview, you display whatever view is currently open on your screen. For example, if you've applied a filter to a view or if you've sorted the items in your project in some way, that's what appears in Print Preview. Figure 6-1 shows the Gantt Chart view for the book-publishing project, and Figure 6-2 shows how the Gantt Chart view appears in Print Preview.

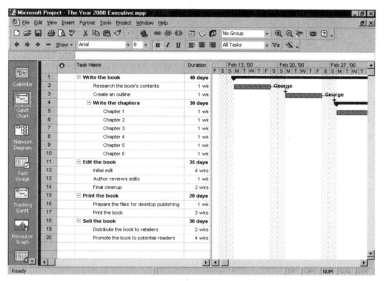

Figure 6-1   The book-publishing project in Gantt Chart view.

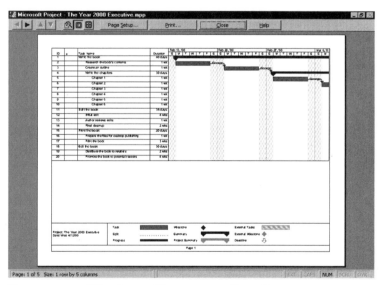

Figure 6-2   The Gantt Chart view in Print Preview.

Figure 6-3   The toolbar buttons in Print Preview.

Figure 6-3 shows the buttons on the Print Preview toolbar. Table 6-1 lists the buttons in order from left to right and explains how you use them to examine what will become your printed output in various levels of detail.

BUTTON	WHAT IT DOES
Page Left	Displays the previous page.
Page Right	Displays the next page.
Page Up	Displays the page above the current page in the printing order.
Page Down	Displays the page below the current page in the printing order.
Zoom	Displays an enlarged view of a portion of the current page.
One Page	Displays only a single page.
Multiple Pages	Displays all the pages of the current view in printing order.
Page Setup	Opens the Page Setup dialog box.
Print	Opens the Print dialog box.
Close	Closes the Print Preview window.
Help	Opens Help for Project.

Table 6-1   The buttons on the Print Preview toolbar.

Figure 6-4 shows how Project displays a multiple-page document when you click the Multiple Pages button. The first row displays, from left to right, pages 1, 3, 5, 7, 9, and 11. Row 2 displays pages 2, 4, 6, 8, and 10.

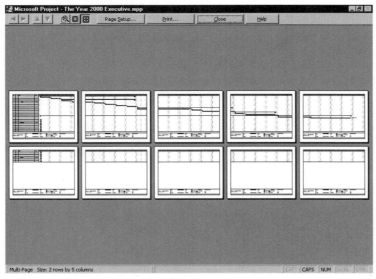

Figure 6-4   A multiple-page document displayed in Print Preview.

Understanding the Page Setup Dialog Box

To exert control over what is printed and how, you use the Page Setup dialog box, which you can open in the following ways:

- By choosing the File menu's Page Setup command
- By clicking the Page Setup button in the Print Preview window

The Page Tab

When you first open the Page Setup dialog box, it displays the Page tab, as shown in Figure 6-5. You use the options on this tab to adjust the paper orientation and the scaling and to specify the paper size and the first page number.

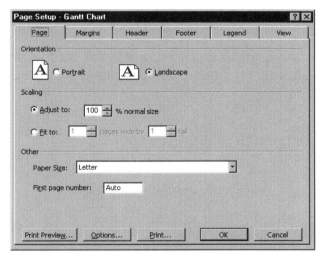

Figure 6-5   The Page tab of the Page Setup dialog box.

In the Orientation section of the Page tab, specify whether you want to print vertically on the page (choose Portrait) or horizontally (choose Landscape).

In the Scaling section, you can specify a percentage of the normal size in which a page would print, and you can click the Fit To button and specify that the document print on only the number of pages you specify. Obviously, the degree to which this is successful depends on the number of pages in the view you want to print.

In the Other section, you can specify a paper size. The default paper size is the one you set up in Windows, but you can specify any of the following that are allowed by your printer:

- Letter (8.5 x 11 in.)
- A4 (210 x 297 mm)
- Legal (8.5 x 14 in.)
- Executive (7.25 x 10.5 in.)
- No. 10 Envelope (4.12 x 9.5 in.)

If you want text other than "Page 1" to print on the first page, enter that in the First Page Number box.

Click the Options button to open a dialog box in which you can specify settings for your particular printer. These may include print quality, color, and so on. You'll find the Options button as well as the Print Preview button and the Print button on each tab in the Page Setup dialog box.

The Margins Tab

You use the options on the Margins tab, which is shown in Figure 6-6, to set left, right, top, and bottom margins and to specify whether you want margins around pages. The default is to print a border around every page. Figure 6-7 shows a page with a surrounding border.

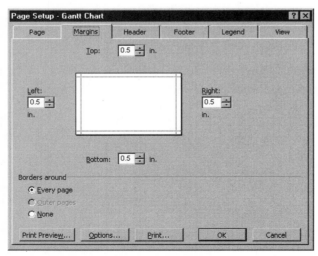

Figure 6-6   The Margins tab of the Page Setup dialog box.

ID	ⓞ	Task Name	Duration	Start	Finish	Predecessors	Resource Names
1		**Write the book**	**40 days**	**Mon 2/14/00**	**Fri 4/7/00**		
2		Research the book's contents	1 wk	Mon 2/14/00	Fri 2/18/00		George
3		Create an outline	1 wk	Mon 2/21/00	Fri 2/25/00	2	George
4		**Write the chapters**	**30 days**	**Mon 2/28/00**	**Fri 4/7/00**	3	
5		Chapter 1	1 wk	Mon 2/28/00	Fri 3/3/00		George
6		Chapter 2	1 wk	Mon 3/6/00	Fri 3/10/00	5	George
7		Chapter 3	1 wk	Mon 3/13/00	Fri 3/17/00	6	George
8		Chapter 4	1 wk	Mon 3/20/00	Fri 3/24/00	7	George
9		Chapter 5	1 wk	Mon 3/27/00	Fri 3/31/00	8	George
10		Chapter 6	1 wk	Mon 4/3/00	Fri 4/7/00	9	George
11		**Edit the book**	**35 days**	**Mon 4/10/00**	**Fri 5/26/00**		
12		Initial edit	4 wks	Mon 4/10/00	Fri 5/5/00	10	Martha
13		Author reviews edits	1 wk	Mon 5/8/00	Fri 5/12/00	12	George
14		Final cleanup	2 wks	Mon 5/15/00	Fri 5/26/00	13	Martha
15		**Print the book**	**20 days**	**Mon 5/29/00**	**Fri 6/23/00**		
16		Prepare the files for desktop publishing	1 wk	Mon 5/29/00	Fri 6/2/00	14	Ben
17		Print the book	3 wks	Mon 6/5/00	Fri 6/23/00	16	Ben
18		**Sell the book**	**30 days**	**Mon 6/26/00**	**Fri 8/4/00**		
19		Distribute the book to retailers	2 wks	Mon 6/26/00	Fri 7/7/00	17	ABC Distributors
20		Promote the book to potential readers	4 wks	Mon 7/10/00	Fri 8/4/00	19	Ace Marketing Associates

Page 1

Figure 6-7   By default, Project prints a border around the edges of every page.

The Header Tab

A header is information that will appear at the top of every printed page in your document. You specify what you want in the header by selecting options on the Header tab, which is shown in Figure 6-8.

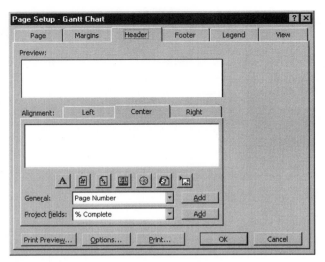

Figure 6-8   The Header tab of the Page Setup dialog box.

You use the buttons on this tab, which are listed in order from left to right in Table 6-2, to insert and format text that you specify in the Selection box. The Sample box shows how the text will appear in the header on the printed page.

BUTTON	WHAT IT DOES
Format Text Font	Opens the Font dialog box so that you can format selected text.
Insert Page Number	Prints a page number in the header.
Insert Total Page Count	Prints the total number of pages in the document.
Insert Current Date	Prints the current date in the header.
Insert Current Time	Prints the current time in the header.
Insert File Time	Prints the filename in the header.
Insert Picture	Opens the Insert Picture dialog box, from which you can select a graphic to include in the header, for example, a logo.

Table 6-2   The buttons on the Header tab.

Depending on the information stored in your project, you can also select other items to print in the header using the General and the Project Fields drop-down list boxes. Select an item, and then click Add.

After you specify the information for the header, click the Format Text Font button to open the Font dialog box, as shown in Figure 6-9. Specify the font, the font style, the font size and color, and whether you want text underlined, and then click OK to apply your choices to the selected text.

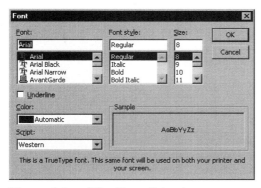

Figure 6-9   The Font dialog box.

The Footer Tab

The Footer tab, which is shown in Figure 6-10, is identical to the Header tab; however, you use the options to select information to display at the bottom of every page rather than at the top. By default, Project prints the word *Page* and the page number in the footer. If you don't want this information in the footer, select it from the Selection box, and press the Delete key.

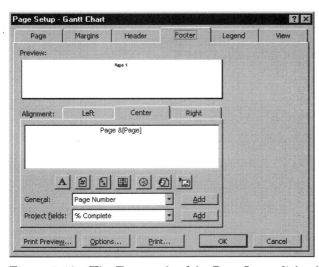

Figure 6-10   The Footer tab of the Page Setup dialog box.

The Legend Tab

The legend describes what the bars and symbols in a chart mean. By default, a printed view contains the following in the legend at the bottom of every page, as well as the name of the project and the current date:

- Task
- Split
- Progress
- Milestone
- Summary
- Project Summary
- External Tasks
- External Milestone
- Deadline

If you look back at Figure 6-7 earlier in this step, you can see the legend at the bottom of the page. Figure 6-11 shows the Legend tab.

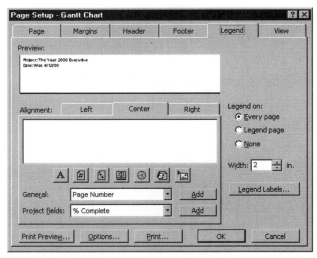

Figure 6-11   The Legend tab of the Page Setup dialog box.

Use the Legend tab to specify whether the legend appears on every page, only on a legend page, or not at all. You can also specify the width of the text portion of the legend in inches, and you can format the text for the legend. To format the text, click the Legend Labels button to open the Font dialog box.

You specify additional text to print in the legend using the same methods as in the Header tab and the Footer tab.

NOTE *The Legend tab is available only when you are printing in Calendar view, Gantt Chart view, or Network Diagram view.*

The View Tab

You use the View tab, as shown in Figure 6-12, to specify whether to print all or some columns, notes, and blank pages and whether to fit the timescale to the end of a page.

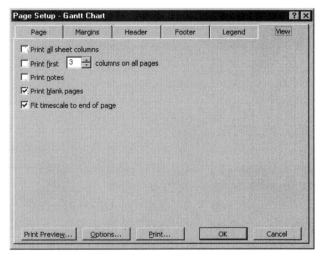

Figure 6-12 The View tab of the Page Setup dialog box.

After you specify all your options in the Page Setup dialog box, you can click OK, or you can click the Print button. Clicking OK displays the current view. Clicking Print opens the Print dialog box.

The Print Dialog Box

You can open the Print dialog box in the following ways:

- By choosing the File menu's Print command
- By clicking the Print button in the Print Preview windows
- By clicking the Print button in the Page Setup dialog box

Regardless of how you open it, the Print dialog box, which is shown in Figure 6-13, will look familiar if you've worked with other Windows applications.

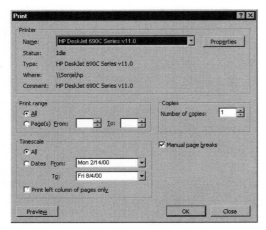

Figure 6-13 The Print dialog box.

If you want to use a printer other than the default, select it in the Name box. To change the settings for your printer, click the Properties button to open the Properties dialog box.

To select what to print, click an option button in the Print Range section. You can print all the pages or only those in the range you specify. Specify the number of copies to print in the Number Of Copies drop-down list box.

NOTE   *In Project, you can't print only a selection, for example, rows 4 through 6.*

In the Timescale section, you can select to print the entire timescale or only a portion within the dates you specify. If you don't want to print the timescale, select the Print Left Column Of Pages Only check box. If you want to break between printed pages at the places you specified, select the Manual Page Breaks check box. If this check box is not checked, Project uses its automatic page breaks.

TIP   *To insert manual page breaks in a printed view, place the cursor where you want the break and then choose the Insert menu's Page Break command.*

When the settings are to your liking, click OK to print your document.

Generating Reports

Although by this time you may have fallen in love with the Network Diagram view or with the Gantt Chart view of your project, printed output of either of these views may make no sense at all to a stakeholder who is not familiar with Project. Your best bet, in this case, is to distribute a standard report that looks similar to what you see in Figure 6-14.

The Year 2000 Executive			
as of Fri 2/11/00			
Dates			
Start:	Mon 2/14/00	Finish:	Fri 8/4/00
Baseline Start:	Mon 2/14/00	Baseline Finish:	Fri 8/4/00
Actual Start:	NA	Actual Finish:	NA
Start Variance:	0 days	Finish Variance:	0 days
Duration			
Scheduled:	125 days	Remaining:	125 days
Baseline:	125 days	Actual:	0 days
Variance:	0 days	Percent Complete:	0%
Work			
Scheduled:	1,000 hrs	Remaining:	1,000 hrs
Baseline:	1,000 hrs	Actual:	0 hrs
Variance:	0 hrs	Percent Complete:	0%
Costs			
Scheduled:	$27,200.00	Remaining:	$27,200.00
Baseline:	$27,200.00	Actual:	$0.00
Variance:	$0.00		
Task Status		**Resource Status**	
Tasks not yet started:	20	Work Resources:	5
Tasks in progress:	0	Overallocated Work Resources:	0
Tasks completed:	0	Material Resources:	0
Total Tasks:	20	Total Resources:	5

Figure 6-14   In Project, you can create a number of standard reports similar to this one.

Table 6-3 lists and describes the predefined reports you can create in Project. Later in this section, you'll see how to create a customized report.

CATEGORY	TYPE	WHAT IT SHOWS
Overview	Project Summary	Top-level information about your projects, including dates, duration, work, costs, task status, and resource status.
	Top-Level Tasks	The highest-level summary tasks as of the current date.
	Critical Tasks	The status of tasks on the critical path.
	Milestones	Information, such as planned duration, start and finish dates, predecessors, and resources, about each milestone.
	Working Days	The base calendar information.
Current Activities	Unstarted Tasks	The tasks that have not yet begun, sorted by start date.
	Tasks Starting Soon	Tasks starting within a date range that you supply.
	Tasks in Progress	Tasks that have started but that are not finished.
	Completed Tasks	All finished tasks, including the actual duration and the actual start and finish dates.
	Should Have Started Tasks	Tasks that should have begun by a date that you specify.
	Slipping Tasks	Tasks that have started which are behind schedule.
Costs	Cash Flow	The costs for weekly time increments by task.
	Budget	All tasks, the budgeted costs, and the variance between budgeted and actual cost.
	Overbudget Tasks	Cost, baseline, variance, and actual information about tasks that exceed budget
	Overbudget Resources	Resources whose cost will exceed budget based on current progress.
	Earned Value	The status of each task's cost when you compare planned to actual cost.

CATEGORY	TYPE	WHAT IT SHOWS
Assignments	Who Does What	Resources and their associated tasks, amount of work planned for each task, planned start and finish dates, and resource notes (if any).
	Who Does What When	Daily work scheduled for each resource on each task.
	To-Do List	The tasks assigned to a resource you select (on a weekly basis).
	Overallocated Resources	The overallocated resources, their tasks, and total hours of work assigned to them.
Workload	Task Usage	Tasks and their assigned resources and the amount of work assigned to each resource (in weekly increments).
	Resource Usage	Resources and the tasks assigned to them and the amount of work assigned to each resource (in weekly increments).

Table 6-3   The types of standard reports in Project.

Using the Reports Dialog Box

To generate a predefined report, take the following actions:

1. Choose the View menu's Reports command.

Project displays the Reports dialog box, as shown in Figure 6-15.

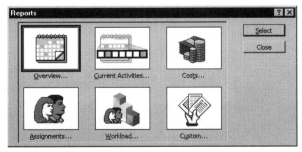

Figure 6-15   The Reports dialog box.

2. Click a report category, and then click the Select button.

Project displays the Reports dialog box for that category. Figure 6-16 shows the Reports dialog box for the Overview category.

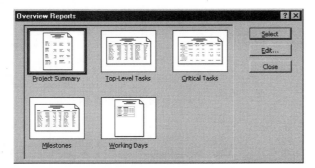

Figure 6-16   The Overview Reports dialog box.

3. Select a report type, and click the Select button.

Project displays the report in Print Preview. Figure 6-17 shows a Project Summary report open in Print Preview.

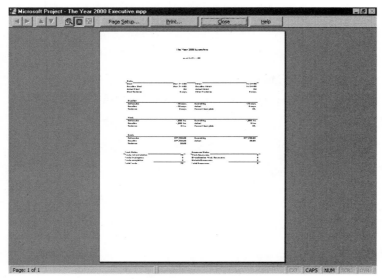

Figure 6-17   The Project Summary report open in Print Preview.

4. To print the report, click the Print button.

Project displays the Print dialog box.

5. Specify whether you want to print all or only selected pages and the number of copies.

Click OK when you're finished.

Understanding the Types of Reports

Table 6-3, earlier in this step, summarizes the categories of reports and the types each contains, as well as gives you an idea of the focus of each report. This section shows you what some sample reports look like.

The Overview Category

Figure 6-18 shows a Critical Tasks report for the book-publishing project.

ID	o	Task Name				Duration	Start	Finish	Predecessors
1		**Write the book**				**40 days**	**Mon 2/14/00**	**Fri 4/7/00**	
2		Research the book's contents				1 wk	Mon 2/14/00	Fri 2/18/00	
		ID	*Successor Name*	*Type*	*Lag*				
		3	*Create an outline*	*FS*	*0 days*				
3		Create an outline				1 wk	Mon 2/21/00	Fri 2/25/00	2
		ID	*Successor Name*	*Type*	*Lag*				
		4	*Write the chapters*	*FS*	*0 days*				
4		**Write the chapters**				**30 days**	**Mon 2/28/00**	**Fri 4/7/00**	3
5		Chapter 1				1 wk	Mon 2/28/00	Fri 3/3/00	
		ID	*Successor Name*	*Type*	*Lag*				
		6	*Chapter 2*	*FS*	*0 days*				
6		Chapter 2				1 wk	Mon 3/6/00	Fri 3/10/00	5
		ID	*Successor Name*	*Type*	*Lag*				
		7	*Chapter 3*	*FS*	*0 days*				
7		Chapter 3				1 wk	Mon 3/13/00	Fri 3/17/00	6
		ID	*Successor Name*	*Type*	*Lag*				
		8	*Chapter 4*	*FS*	*0 days*				
8		Chapter 4				1 wk	Mon 3/20/00	Fri 3/24/00	7
		ID	*Successor Name*	*Type*	*Lag*				
		9	*Chapter 5*	*FS*	*0 days*				
9		Chapter 5				1 wk	Mon 3/27/00	Fri 3/31/00	8
		ID	*Successor Name*	*Type*	*Lag*				
		10	*Chapter 6*	*FS*	*0 days*				
10		Chapter 6				1 wk	Mon 4/3/00	Fri 4/7/00	9
		ID	*Successor Name*	*Type*	*Lag*				
		12	*Initial edit*	*FS*	*0 days*				
11		**Edit the book**				**35 days**	**Mon 4/10/00**	**Fri 5/26/00**	
12		Initial edit				4 wks	Mon 4/10/00	Fri 5/5/00	10
		ID	*Successor Name*	*Type*	*Lag*				
		13	*Author reviews edits*	*FS*	*0 days*				
13		Author reviews edits				1 wk	Mon 5/8/00	Fri 5/12/00	12
		ID	*Successor Name*	*Type*	*Lag*				
		14	*Final cleanup*	*FS*	*0 days*				
14		Final cleanup				2 wks	Mon 5/15/00	Fri 5/26/00	13
		ID	*Successor Name*		*Type*	*Lag*				
		16	*Prepare the files for desktop publishing*		*FS*	*0 days*				
15		**Print the book**				**20 days**	**Mon 5/29/00**	**Fri 6/23/00**	
16		Prepare the files for desktop publishing				1 wk	Mon 5/29/00	Fri 6/2/00	14
		ID	*Successor Name*	*Type*	*Lag*				
		17	*Print the book*	*FS*	*0 days*				

Page 1

Figure 6-18   A Critical Tasks report.

Current Activities

As you can see from Table 6-3, you can specify dates for the Tasks Starting Soon report and the Should Have Started report in this category. Figure 6-19 shows the Tasks Starting Soon report for the book-publishing project.

Tasks Starting Soon as of Fri 2/11/00
The Year 2000 Executive

ID	ο	Task Name	Duration	Start	Finish	Predecessors
5		Chapter 1	1 wk	Mon 2/28/00	Fri 3/3/00	
	ID	Resource Name	Units	Work	Delay	Start	Finish
	1	George	100%	40 hrs	0 days	Mon 2/28/00	Fri 3/3/00
6		Chapter 2	1 wk	Mon 3/6/00	Fri 3/10/00	5
	ID	Resource Name	Units	Work	Delay	Start	Finish
	1	George	100%	40 hrs	0 days	Mon 3/6/00	Fri 3/10/00
7		Chapter 3	1 wk	Mon 3/13/00	Fri 3/17/00	6
	ID	Resource Name	Units	Work	Delay	Start	Finish
	1	George	100%	40 hrs	0 days	Mon 3/13/00	Fri 3/17/00
8		Chapter 4	1 wk	Mon 3/20/00	Fri 3/24/00	7
	ID	Resource Name	Units	Work	Delay	Start	Finish
	1	George	100%	40 hrs	0 days	Mon 3/20/00	Fri 3/24/00
9		Chapter 5	1 wk	Mon 3/27/00	Fri 3/31/00	8
	ID	Resource Name	Units	Work	Delay	Start	Finish
	1	George	100%	40 hrs	0 days	Mon 3/27/00	Fri 3/31/00
10		Chapter 6	1 wk	Mon 4/3/00	Fri 4/7/00	9
	ID	Resource Name	Units	Work	Delay	Start	Finish
	1	George	100%	40 hrs	0 days	Mon 4/3/00	Fri 4/7/00
12		Initial edit	4 wks	Mon 4/10/00	Fri 5/5/00	10
	ID	Resource Name	Units	Work	Delay	Start	Finish
	2	Martha	100%	160 hrs	0 days	Mon 4/10/00	Fri 5/5/00
13		Author reviews edits	1 wk	Mon 5/8/00	Fri 5/12/00	12
	ID	Resource Name	Units	Work	Delay	Start	Finish
	1	George	100%	40 hrs	0 days	Mon 5/8/00	Fri 5/12/00
14		Final cleanup	2 wks	Mon 5/15/00	Fri 5/26/00	13
	ID	Resource Name	Units	Work	Delay	Start	Finish
	2	Martha	100%	80 hrs	0 days	Mon 5/15/00	Fri 5/26/00
16		Prepare the files for desktop publishing	1 wk	Mon 5/29/00	Fri 6/2/00	14
	ID	Resource Name	Units	Work	Delay	Start	Finish
	3	Ben	100%	40 hrs	0 days	Mon 5/29/00	Fri 6/2/00
17		Print the book	3 wks	Mon 6/5/00	Fri 6/23/00	16
	ID	Resource Name	Units	Work	Delay	Start	Finish
	3	Ben	100%	120 hrs	0 days	Mon 6/5/00	Fri 6/23/00

Figure 6-19   A Tasks Starting Soon report.

To create a Tasks Starting Soon report, take the following actions:

1. **Choose the View menu's Reports command.**

   Project displays the Reports dialog box.

2. **Click Current Activities, and click the Select button.**

   Project displays the Current Activity Reports dialog box, as shown in Figure 6-20.

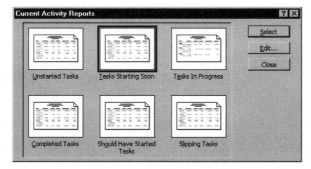

Figure 6-20   The Current Activity Reports dialog box.

3. **Click Tasks Starting Soon, and click the Select button.**

   Project displays the first Date Range dialog box, as shown in Figure 6-21.

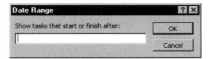

Figure 6-21   The Date Range dialog box.

4. Enter a date for which you want to show tasks that start or finish after.

5. Enter a start or a finish date, and click OK.

Project displays a second Date Range box.

6. Enter a date that you want tasks to finish before, and click OK.

Your Tasks Starting Soon report opens in Print Preview.

Assignments

Especially if you have a long, complex project, you might want to print out a to-do list for each project participant. Figure 6-22 shows such a list for George, the writer in the book-publishing project.

	To Do List as of Fri 2/11/00 The Year 2000 Executive				
ID ₀	**Task Name**	**Duration**	**Start**	**Finish**	**Predecessors**
Week of February 13					
2	Research the book's contents	1 wk	Mon 2/14/00	Fri 2/18/00	
Week of February 20					
3	Create an outline	1 wk	Mon 2/21/00	Fri 2/25/00	2
Week of February 27					
5	Chapter 1	1 wk	Mon 2/28/00	Fri 3/3/00	
Week of March 5					
6	Chapter 2	1 wk	Mon 3/6/00	Fri 3/10/00	5
Week of March 12					
7	Chapter 3	1 wk	Mon 3/13/00	Fri 3/17/00	6
Week of March 19					
8	Chapter 4	1 wk	Mon 3/20/00	Fri 3/24/00	7
Week of March 26					
9	Chapter 5	1 wk	Mon 3/27/00	Fri 3/31/00	8
Week of April 2					
10	Chapter 6	1 wk	Mon 4/3/00	Fri 4/7/00	9
Week of May 7					
13	Author reviews edits	1 wk	Mon 5/8/00	Fri 5/12/00	12

Figure 6-22   A To-Do List report.

To generate the To-Do List reports, take the following actions:

1. Open the Project file.

2. Choose the View menu's Reports command.

Project displays the Reports dialog box.

3. Click Assignments, and then click the Select button.

Project displays the Assignment Reports dialog box, as shown in Figure 6-23.

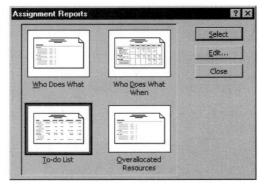

Figure 6-23   The Assignment Reports dialog box.

4. Click To-Do List, and click the Select button.

Project displays the Using Resource dialog box, as shown in Figure 6-24.

Figure 6-24   The Using Resource dialog box.

5. Click the down arrow, select a resource, and then click OK.

Your To-Do List report opens in Print Preview.

Customizing a Report

As you can see from the preceding examples, the reports in Project are nicely arranged and formatted, but you can also customize a report's appearance. To do so, take the following actions:

1. Choose the View menu's Reports command.

Project displays the Reports dialog box.

2. Click Custom, and then click the Select button.

Project displays the Custom Reports dialog box, as shown in Figure 6-25.

Figure 6-25   The Custom Reports dialog box.

3. Select a report from the Reports list, and then click the Edit button.

For the Project Summary and Base Calendar reports, Project displays the Report Text dialog box, as shown in Figure 6-26. Select an item in the Item To Change list. Choose a font, a font style, a font size and color, and specify whether you want the item underlined, and then click OK.

For all other reports, Project displays the Report dialog box for that type. On the Definition tab, you can rename the report, select a different time period, or change the report's table or filter. On the Details tab, you can specify the information you want to include in your report. On the Sort tab, you can select the sort order for the report.

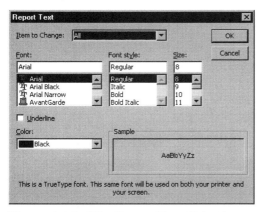

Figure 6-26   The Report Text dialog box.

4. In the Custom Reports dialog box, click the Print button to print the report or click the Preview button if you want to check your formatting before printing.

For some reports, all you can change is the formatting, but for other reports you can change the table, the task, or the resource filter to create a new type of report.

Creating a Report from an Existing Report

To create a report from an existing report, take the following actions:

1. **Choose the View menu's Reports command.**

   Project displays the Reports dialog box.

2. **Click Custom, and then click the Select button.**

   Project displays the Custom Reports dialog box.

3. **Select a report from the Reports list, and then click the New button.**

   Project displays the Define New Report dialog box, as shown in Figure 6-27.

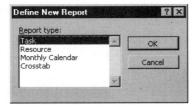

Figure 6-27   The Define New Report dialog box.

4. **Select a type from the Report Type list, and click OK.**

   Project displays the Report dialog box for that type. Figure 6-28 shows the Report dialog box for the Task type.

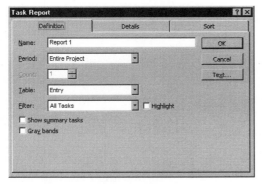

Figure 6-28   The Definition tab of the Task Report dialog box.

5. On the Definition tab, give the report a name, select a time period, and change the report's table or filter.

6. On the Details tab, select check boxes to specify the information you want to include in your report.

Figure 6-29 shows this tab.

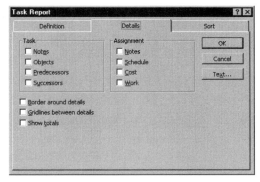

Figure 6-29 The Details tab of the Task Report dialog box.

7. On the Sort tab, select the sort order for the report.

Figure 6-30 shows this tab.

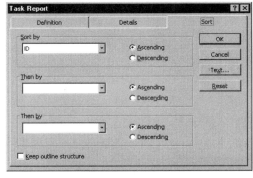

Figure 6-30 The Sort tab of the Task Report dialog box.

8. If you want to reformat any items, click the Text button.

Project displays the Text Styles dialog box where you can reformat items. When you're finished, click OK.

9. Click OK again on the Sort tab, and then click the Print button in the Custom Reports dialog box.

Project prints your newly created report.

Exporting Project Information to Other Applications

When you export Project information, you save it in a format that another application can read and use. For example, you might want to save cost information as a Microsoft Excel worksheet so that someone could work with it in that format.

You can export Project information in a couple of ways:

- By using the Analyze Timescaled Data Wizard
- By saving the information in the format of the other application and then mapping it

First, we'll look at how to use the AnalyzeTimescaled Data Wizard, and then we'll look at how to export Project information to Excel, Microsoft Access, and HTML using one of the predefined export maps. You use an export map to define the information you want to export and to describe how to associate the information in the Project file with information in the other application's file.

Next, we'll look at how you can create a new export map, and then we'll describe how to export Project information to a Microsoft Word file using the Copy and Paste commands and how to create a graphic image from Project information.

Exporting to Excel

To export Project information to Excel, take the following actions:

1. In Project, open the file that you want to export.

2. Choose the File menu's Save As command.

   Project displays the Save As dialog box, as shown in Figure 6-31.

Figure 6-31　The Save As dialog box.

3. Select a folder in which to save the file.

Either accept the filename that Project proposes or type a new filename in the File Name box.

4. Select Microsoft Excel Workbook (*.xls) from the Save As Type drop-down list box, and then click the Save button.

Project displays the Export Mapping dialog box, as shown in Figure 6-32.

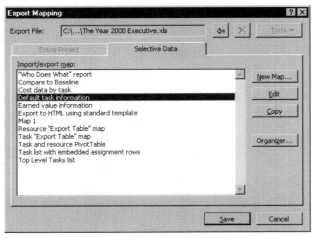

Figure 6-32　The Export Mapping dialog box.

NOTE　*You can also save the file as an Excel PivotTable, which creates two worksheets— one for the data and one for the PivotTable.*

5. Select a map from the Import/Export Map list, and click the Save button.

Figure 6-33 shows the book-publishing project in Gantt Chart view in Project, and Figure 6-34 shows the task information as it appears when exported to an Excel worksheet.

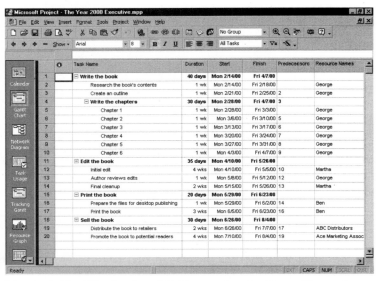

Figure 6-33   The book-publishing project in Gantt Chart view.

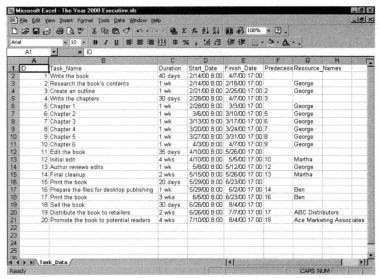

Figure 6-34   Task information about the book-publishing project open in Excel.

Exporting to Access

To export Project information to Access, take the following actions:

1. In Project, open the file you want to export.

2. Choose the File menu's Save As command.

Project displays the Save As dialog box.

3. Select a folder in which to save the file.

Either accept the filename that Project proposes or type a new filename in the File Name box.

4. Select Microsoft Access Databases (*.mdb) from the Save As Type drop-down list box, and then click the Save button.

Project displays the Save To Database dialog box, as shown in Figure 6-35.

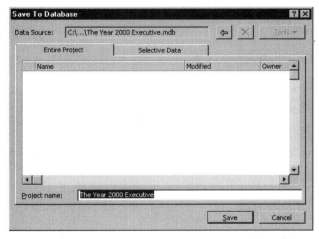

Figure 6-35   The Entire Project tab of the Save To Database dialog box.

5. To export all the data in your project, click the Save button.

Project exports all the data in the project.

6. To export only selected data, click the Selective Data tab.

Figure 6-36 shows this tab.

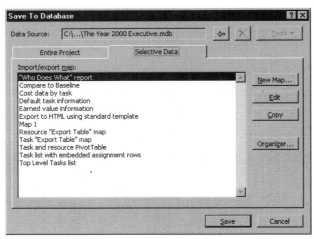

Figure 6-36   The Selective Data tab of the Save To Database dialog box.

7. From the Import/Export Map list, select the map you want to use for importing the data.

Click the Save button when you're finished. Project exports the data you specified.

Exporting to HTML

You can save a Project file as a web page that can then be opened in a browser such as Microsoft Internet Explorer. Take the following actions:

1. Open the file that you want to save as a web page.

2. Choose the File menu's Save As Web Page command.

Project opens the Save As dialog box, as shown in Figure 6-37, and selects the Web Page (*.html; *.htm) file type.

Figure 6-37   The Save As dialog box for saving a Project file as a web page.

3. **Click the Save button.**

Project displays the Export Mapping dialog box.

4. **Select the Export To HTML Using Standard Template map, and click the Save button.**

Figure 6-38 shows the book-publishing project open in Internet Explorer. Choose the View menu's Source command to see the HTML for the file.

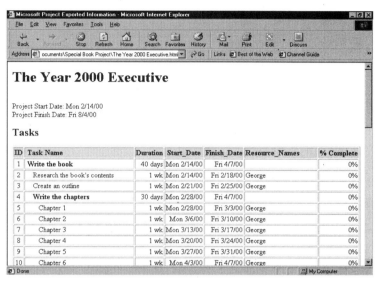

Figure 6-38 Project information saved as an HTML file and open in Internet Explorer.

Creating a New Export Map

If none of the existing export maps suit your needs, you can create a new one. In the following example, we'll create a new export map for a file to be exported into Excel, but the steps are essentially the same regardless of the application to which you want to export. You would simply see options specific to that program.

To create a new export map, take the following actions:

1. **In Project, open the file you want to export.**

2. **Choose the File menu's Save As command.**

Project displays the Save As dialog box.

3. **Select a folder in which to save the file.**

   Either accept the filename that Project proposes or type a new filename in the File Name box.

4. **Select Microsoft Excel Workbook (*.xls) from the Save As Type drop-down list box, and then click the Save button.**

   Project displays the Export Mapping dialog box.

5. **Click the New Map button.**

   Project displays the Define Import/Export Map dialog box, as shown in Figure 6-39.

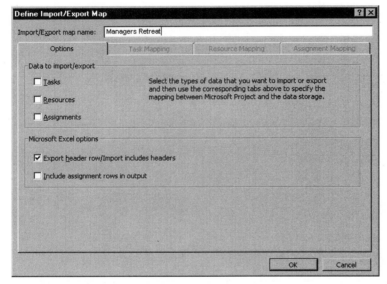

Figure 6-39   The Options tab of the Define Import/Export Map dialog box.

6. **On the Options tab, select the type of data you want to import, and then select the corresponding tab to specify the mapping.**

   Figure 6-40 shows the Task Mapping tab, but the options are the same on the Resource Mapping and Assignment Mapping tabs.

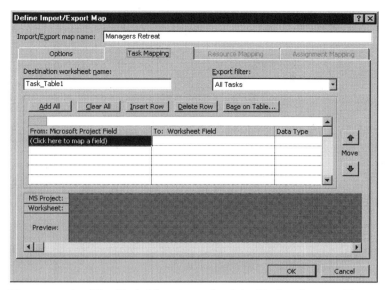

Figure 6-40 The Task Mapping tab of the Define Import/Export Map dialog box.

7. **In the Destination Worksheet Name box, accept the name that Project suggests or type another one.**

8. **In the Export Filter drop-down list box, select the task that you want to export.**

9. **To add fields one at a time, click (Click Here To Map A Field).**

   Select the fields you want to add individually from the drop-down list.

10. **Click in the To: Worksheet Field column in the next cell.**

    Project suggests a field name, but you can change it if you want.

    As you add fields, the Preview box shows you how they will display in Excel.

NOTE *To add all the fields in the Project file at once, click the Add All button. To clear all the fields and start over, click the Clear All button. To insert or delete a row, click the appropriate button.*

11. **If you want to base your map on a table, click the Base On Table button.**

    Project displays the Select Base Table For Field Mapping dialog box, as shown in Figure 6-41.

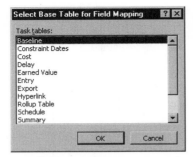

Figure 6-41   The Select Base Table For Field Mapping dialog box.

Select a table from the Task Tables list, and click OK.

12. **When you've finished mapping fields, click OK.**

Project displays the Export Mapping dialog box, which now shows the name of the new map in the Import/Export Map list.

13. **To export the file, click the Save button.**

Click Close to save the map but cancel the export operation.

Sending to Word

You can't export Project information to Word, but you can select information and then copy it to a Word document. To do so, take the following actions:

1. **In Project, open the file that contains the information you want to copy.**

2. **Select the information, and press Ctrl+C.**

This copies the information to the Clipboard.

3. **Open the Word document, and position the cursor where you want to copy the information.**

To paste the Project data into a blank Word document, create a new document by clicking the New toolbar button.

4. **Press Ctrl+V.**

Figure 6-42 shows the Entry table for the book-publishing project in Gantt Chart view. Figure 6-43 shows how the Task Name, Duration, Start, and Finish columns appear when copied into Word. In Word, you can convert the tab-separated columns to a table.

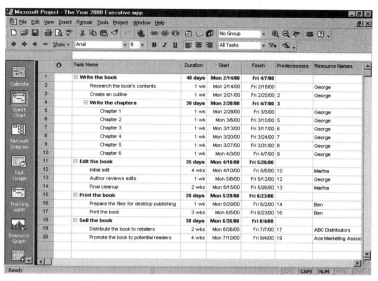

Figure 6-42   The Entry table for the book-publishing project in Gantt Chart view in Project.

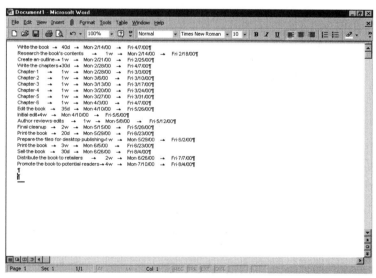

Figure 6-43   The Project information after it has been copied into Word.

Copying Project Information to a Graphics File

In addition to all the other neat ways that you can manipulate your Project information, you can copy it to a graphics file that can be displayed on a computer screen or that can be printed, and you can save the graphics file as a Graphics Interchange File (GIF) that you can open and change in an image-editing program and insert on a web page. To do this, take the following actions:

1. **Open the file, and select the view of which you want a picture.**

   If you want to copy only a portion of the current display, select that portion.

2. **Click the Copy Picture toolbar button.**

   The Copy Picture button looks like a little camera. Project displays the Copy Picture dialog box, as shown in Figure 6-44.

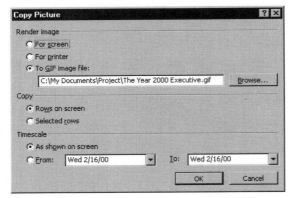

Figure 6-44   The Copy Picture dialog box.

3. **In the Render Image section, select the type of image you want.**

NOTE   *If you selected rows before you opened the Copy Picture dialog box, click the Selected Rows option button.*

4. **Specify the range of dates over which you want the data included in the image.**

   To copy information for a range of dates other than what is currently displayed, enter the dates in the From and To boxes.

5. **Click OK to save your Project information as a picture.**

   Figure 6-45 shows a GIF image created from information in the book-publishing project and open in Paint.

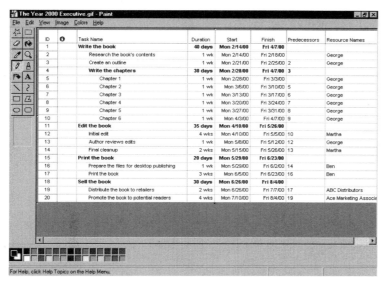

Figure 6-45 A GIF image of part of a project open in Paint.

Summary

In this step, you've been introduced to three ways that you can present Project information to stakeholders: (1) by distributing printed views; (2) by generating and printing reports; and (3) by exporting Project information into other applications so that stakeholders can access it there. If you're in the beginning stage of a project, the next step in the process may be to get approval for your project. Once you do so, you're off and running, and the next step is to monitor the project—its schedule and costs and how what is actually being done compares with your plan. The next step, "Step 7: Manage Project Progress," shows you how to update your project to reflect what's actually taking place.

Step 7

MANAGE PROJECT PROGRESS

Tasks Required to Complete the Step

- Establishing and using a baseline
- Updating tasks
- Updating the schedule
- Setting and updating costs
- Comparing your progress with your plan
- Performing earned value analysis

If you've completed the previous six steps, you're ready to start tracking the progress of your project. Well, almost. Step 4 discusses how to estimate resource costs, but doesn't discuss how to estimate task costs, how to record costs, and how to compare actual costs with estimated costs. The latter part of this step covers these topics.

First, however, we need to look at how you can use a baseline to monitor your progress and how you can record actual information about your schedule and tasks.

Establishing and Using a Baseline

A baseline, as you'll recall from Step 4, is a picture of your final project plan before the start date. You can choose whether or not to save your project with a baseline, but if you do, you can use the baseline as a point of reference when monitoring your project.

Setting the Baseline

As you may also recall, the first time you save a project, the Planning Wizard asks whether you want to save a baseline for the project. You will most likely want to save your project several times before saving the baseline and will want to wait until the final planning stages are complete to save the baseline. Thus, you might want to click the Don't Tell Me About This Again check box, as shown in Figure 7-1, to avoid the annoyance of seeing this dialog box every time you save your project. Don't worry—you have another way to save the baseline when you're ready.

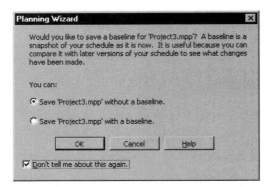

Figure 7-1   The Planning Wizard dialog box.

To save the baseline without using the Planning Wizard, take the following actions:

1. Choose the Tools menu's Tracking command, and then choose the submenu's Save Baseline command.

Project displays the Save Baseline dialog box, as shown in Figure 7-2.

Figure 7-2   The Save Baseline dialog box.

2. If necessary, click the Save Baseline option button, and then click OK.

Your other option in the Save Baseline dialog box is to save an interim plan, which you might want to do if your project gets terribly off track. For example, perhaps it starts three months later than you expected. It's important to retain your original baseline because it shows your initial planning, but you also need a way to track your project that is more in line with reality.

Normally, you'll want to save an interim plan only for tasks that haven't been started. To save an interim plan, take the following actions:

1. Open your project, and select the tasks that have not yet started.

2. Choose the Tools menu's Tracking command, and then choose the submenu's Save Baseline command.

   Project displays the Save Baseline dialog box.

3. Click the Save Interim Plan option button.

4. In the Copy field, click the drop-down arrow, and select a current start to finish setting.

5. In the Into field, click the drop-down arrow, and select an interim item.

WARNING *Don't select the Baseline Start/Finish item in either the Copy field or the Into field. Doing so overwrites your original baseline.*

6. Click the Selected Tasks option button, and then click OK.

To clear a baseline or an interim plan, choose the Tools menu's Tracking command, and then choose the submenu's Clear Baseline command to open the Clear Baseline dialog box, as shown in Figure 7-3. Select what you want to clear, and click OK.

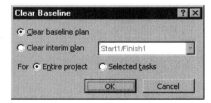

Figure 7-3   The Clear Baseline dialog box.

Changing the Baseline

In general, you don't want to change the baseline, but in certain cases it will be necessary. For example, perhaps you realize after you're into the project that a single task is really two tasks that must be done by two people. To add or modify tasks, use the Entry table in Gantt Chart view, select the tasks, and then save them in the Save Baseline dialog box, following the actions described in the previous section.

Updating Tasks

Before we get into the mechanics of how you update tasks to show what is actually taking place with your project, we need to take a look at the Tracking toolbar, which you can use to quickly enter some common updates. To display the Tracking toolbar, right-click any place in the toolbar area, and select Tracking. Figure 7-4 shows the Tracking toolbar, which contains the following buttons, in left-to-right order:

- Project Statistics
- Update As Scheduled
- Reschedule Work
- Add Progress Line
- 0% Complete
- 25% Complete
- 50% Complete
- 75% Complete
- 100% Complete
- Update Tasks
- Workgroup Toolbar

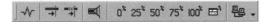

Figure 7-4   The Tracking toolbar.

NOTE   *You'll find information about workgroups in "Step 8: Communicate Project Status."*

Now let's use the Tracking toolbar to enter information about the percentage of tasks complete. Take the following actions:

1. **Open the project in Gantt Chart view.**

2. **Press and hold down the Shift key, and select the task or tasks you want to update.**

   Do this by clicking their names in the Task Name column.

3. **Click one of the % Complete buttons on the Tracking toolbar.**

Figure 7-5 shows the book-publishing project with some updated information about the tasks assigned to George. Suppose that George has finished his research and has created the outline. He has started writing chapter 1 and has about 25 percent of it done. As you can see, a check mark beside items 2 and 3 indicates that those tasks are 100 percent complete. The chart shows a dark line through those bars that represent completed or partially completed tasks.

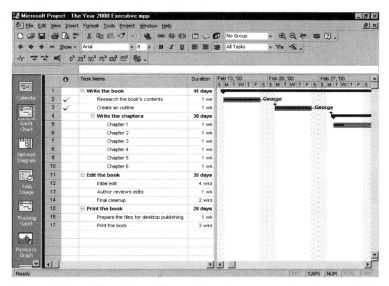

Figure 7-5   The Gantt Chart view shows completed or partially completed tasks.

NOTE   *When you enter a percentage complete for a task, Project updates an actual duration, a remaining duration, and an actual work value.*

Updating the Schedule

As you know, the Gantt Chart view displays your estimated start and finish dates and the durations for tasks. To enter information about how your schedule is actually progressing, you use the Task Details Form view and the Update Tasks dialog box.

Recording Actual Start and Finish Dates

To record the actual dates on which a task starts and finishes, take the following actions:

1. **Open your project in Gantt Chart view.**

2. **Choose the Window menu's Split command.**

    Project displays the Task Form view, as shown in Figure 7-6.

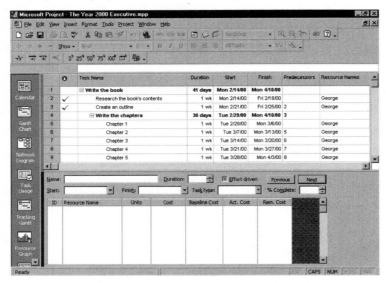

Figure 7-6   The book-publishing project open in combination view.

3. **Click in the bottom pane, and then click the More Views icon on the View Bar.**

    Project displays the More Views dialog box.

4. **Select Task Details Form from the View list, and then click the Apply button.**

    Now your combination view will show the Gantt Chart view in the top pane and the Task Details form in the bottom pane, as shown in Figure 7-7.

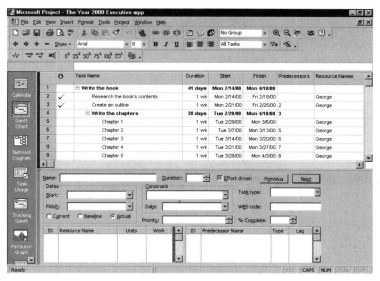

Figure 7-7   The Task Details form is displayed in the bottom pane.

5. **Select a task in the top pane.**

   Project displays information about that task in the Task Details form.

6. **Click the Actual option button.**

   Record an actual start or finish date or both.

7. **Click OK.**

TIP   *To remove the split, choose the Window menu's Remove Split command.*

Recording Actual Durations

You can use the Task Details form to set the actual duration, or you can set the actual duration of a task by clicking the Update Tasks button on the Tracking toolbar and recording information in the Update Tasks dialog box. To use this dialog box, take the following actions:

1. **In Gantt Chart view, select the task that you want to update, and click the Update Tasks button.**

   Project displays the Update Tasks dialog box, as shown in Figure 7-8.

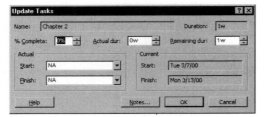

Figure 7-8   The Update Tasks dialog box.

2. **Fill in information such as the percentage of work completed and the actual and remaining duration, and click OK.**

Setting and Updating Costs

Project allows you to assign costs to resources and tasks. You can then total these costs to estimate those project costs that you can directly connect to either a resource or task.

NOTE   *Project doesn't really provide a good way of estimating indirect costs—those costs that aren't directly connected to a task or resource. Project also doesn't provide any way to estimate overhead costs—those costs that aren't directly connected to the project and that are only tangentially related. If you want to include these other costs in your cost estimates—and presumably you do—you need to separately account for them.*

Estimating Task Costs

To estimate task costs, you first need to schedule the project, as described in Step 3, and then identify your resources and estimate the resource costs, as described in Step 4.

After you've done this, you can estimate the costs associated with a task by taking the following actions:

1. **Display the Cost table.**

First, display the project in the Gantt Chart view. Then, choose the View menu's Table command and choose the submenu's Cost command. Project displays the tasks of the project, showing the estimated costs of each, as shown in Figure 7-9.

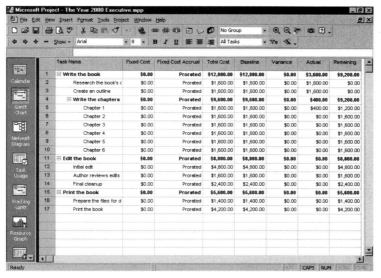

		Task Name	Fixed Cost	Fixed Cost Accrual	Total Cost	Baseline	Variance	Actual	Remaining
	1	⊟ Write the book	$0.00	Prorated	$12,800.00	$12,800.00	$0.00	$3,600.00	$9,200.00
	2	Research the book's c	$0.00	Prorated	$1,600.00	$1,600.00	$0.00	$1,600.00	$0.00
	3	Create an outline	$0.00	Prorated	$1,600.00	$1,600.00	$0.00	$1,600.00	$0.00
	4	⊟ Write the chapters	$0.00	Prorated	$9,600.00	$9,600.00	$0.00	$400.00	$9,200.00
	5	Chapter 1	$0.00	Prorated	$1,600.00	$1,600.00	$0.00	$400.00	$1,200.00
	6	Chapter 2	$0.00	Prorated	$1,600.00	$1,600.00	$0.00	$0.00	$1,600.00
	7	Chapter 3	$0.00	Prorated	$1,600.00	$1,600.00	$0.00	$0.00	$1,600.00
	8	Chapter 4	$0.00	Prorated	$1,600.00	$1,600.00	$0.00	$0.00	$1,600.00
	9	Chapter 5	$0.00	Prorated	$1,600.00	$1,600.00	$0.00	$0.00	$1,600.00
	10	Chapter 6	$0.00	Prorated	$1,600.00	$1,600.00	$0.00	$0.00	$1,600.00
	11	⊟ Edit the book	$0.00	Prorated	$8,800.00	$8,800.00	$0.00	$0.00	$8,800.00
	12	Initial edit	$0.00	Prorated	$4,800.00	$4,800.00	$0.00	$0.00	$4,800.00
	13	Author reviews edits	$0.00	Prorated	$1,600.00	$1,600.00	$0.00	$0.00	$1,600.00
	14	Final cleanup	$0.00	Prorated	$2,400.00	$2,400.00	$0.00	$0.00	$2,400.00
	15	⊟ Print the book	$0.00	Prorated	$5,600.00	$5,600.00	$0.00	$0.00	$5,600.00
	16	Prepare the files for d	$0.00	Prorated	$1,400.00	$1,400.00	$0.00	$0.00	$1,400.00
	17	Print the book	$0.00	Prorated	$4,200.00	$4,200.00	$0.00	$0.00	$4,200.00

Figure 7-9   The Cost table.

The estimated resource costs associated with each task will already show. In Figure 7-9, for example, the Write book task shows a total cost of $12,800. This amount is calculated by totaling the costs of using the resource.

2. Select the first task for which you want to provide additional cost data.

You can select the task by clicking. You can also use the arrow keys.

3. Provide any fixed cost associated with the task.

Click the Fixed Cost box, and then enter any fixed cost associated with this task.

4. Indicate when the fixed cost is incurred.

Use the Fixed Cost Accrual box to indicate when you will incur the fixed cost. The box provides three options: Start, Prorated, and End. Select Start if you incur the fixed cost when the task starts. Select End if you incur the fixed cost when the task ends. Select Prorated if you incur the fixed cost proportionally over the time the task takes.

5. Describe the other task costs in the project, as necessary.

Repeat actions 2 through 4 to describe each of the other task's costs in the project.

As you enter your fixed costs estimates, Project updates the values shown in the Total Cost column, as shown in Figure 7-10.

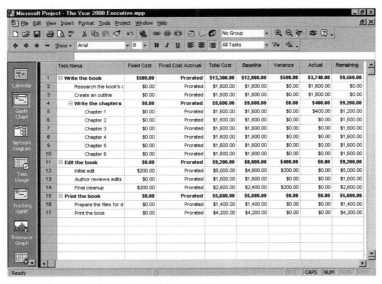

Figure 7-10   The updated Cost table.

Reviewing Estimated Project Costs

Once you've estimated the costs of using a resource and any fixed costs associated with tasks, you can view your estimated costs in several useful ways using Project's cost reports.

NOTE   *One other useful tool, of course, is the Cost table, as shown in Figure 7-10.*

To view Project's cost reports, take the following actions:

1. Choose the View menu's Reports command.

Project displays the Reports dialog box, as shown in Figure 7-11.

Figure 7-11   The Reports dialog box.

2. Choose the Costs category.

To do this, click Costs and then click the Select button. Project displays the Cost Reports dialog box, as shown in Figure 7-12.

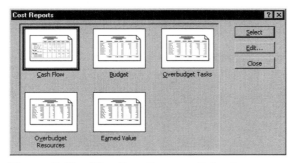

Figure 7-12   The Cost Reports dialog box.

3. Select a cost report.

To see a report, click it and then click the Select button. Project produces an on-screen version of the report. Figure 7-13, for example, shows a Cash Flow report, which shows the cash flows that stem from the costs you estimated for the resources and the costs.

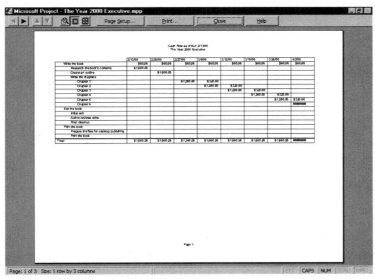

Figure 7-13   The Cash Flow report in a Print Preview window.

As you recall from Step 6, the Project Print Preview window works like the Print Preview window in other Microsoft Windows programs. To print a cost report, click the Print button. To zoom in and out, click the report. To page through a report, click the Page Right, Page Left, Page Up, and Page Down buttons that appear in the upper left corner of the window and are marked with arrowheads.

Figure 7-14, for another example, shows a Budget report. It reports on the total estimated costs of each task.

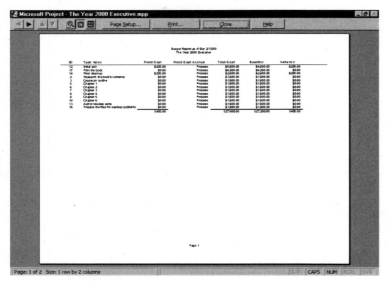

Figure 7-14　The Budget report in a Print Preview window.

Recording Actual Costs

To track actual costs with Project, take the following actions:

1. Display the Cost table.

To do this, first display the project in the Gantt Chart view. Then choose the View menu's Table command, and choose the submenu's Cost command. Project displays the tasks of the project, showing the estimated costs of each, as shown in Figure 7-15.

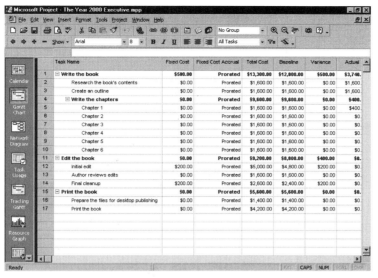

Figure 7-15   The Cost table.

The Cost table will already be familiar to you if you've used Project to estimate project costs. And, in fact, an advantage of using Project both to estimate costs and track actual costs is that you can then compare budgeted amounts with actual amounts.

NOTE   *Step 4 explains how to estimate resource project costs with Project, and the earlier section "Estimating Task Costs" explains how to estimate task costs.*

2. Select the first task for which you want to record actual cost data.

You can select the task by clicking. You can also use the arrow keys.

3. Record the actual costs associated with the task.

Click the Actual Cost box, and then enter the actual costs associated with this task.

NOTE   *You cannot record actual costs for a project unless the task is 100% complete. Note, too, that for tasks that aren't 100% complete, Project estimates the actual costs by multiplying the budgeted costs for the task by the completed percentage for the task. When you mark a task as 100% complete, Project fills in the actual cost with the planned cost. If the actual cost is different from the planned cost, then you'll need to adjust it.*

4. Describe the other actual task costs in the project, as necessary.

Repeat actions 2 and 3 to record the actual costs of each of the other task's costs in the project.

As you record your actual costs, Project updates the values shown in the Total Cost column, as shown in Figure 7-16.

	Task Name	Fixed Cost	Fixed Cost Accrual	Total Cost	Baseline	Variance	Actual	Remai
1	⊟ Write the book	$500.00	Prorated	$13,500.00	$12,800.00	$700.00	$5,605.00	$7,8
2	Research the book's contents	$0.00	Prorated	$1,600.00	$1,600.00	$0.00	$1,600.00	
3	Create an outline	$0.00	Prorated	$1,600.00	$1,600.00	$0.00	$1,600.00	
4	⊟ Write the chapters	$0.00	Prorated	$9,800.00	$9,600.00	$200.00	$2,200.00	$7,6
5	Chapter 1	$0.00	Prorated	$1,600.00	$1,600.00	$0.00	$400.00	$1,2
6	Chapter 2	$200.00	Prorated	$1,800.00	$1,600.00	$200.00	$1,800.00	
7	Chapter 3	$0.00	Prorated	$1,600.00	$1,600.00	$0.00	$0.00	$1,6
8	Chapter 4	$0.00	Prorated	$1,600.00	$1,600.00	$0.00	$0.00	$1,6
9	Chapter 5	$0.00	Prorated	$1,600.00	$1,600.00	$0.00	$0.00	$1,6
10	Chapter 6	$0.00	Prorated	$1,600.00	$1,600.00	$0.00	$0.00	$1,6
11	⊟ Edit the book	$0.00	Prorated	$9,200.00	$8,800.00	$400.00	$0.00	$9,2
12	Initial edit	$200.00	Prorated	$5,000.00	$4,800.00	$200.00	$0.00	$5,0
13	Author reviews edits	$0.00	Prorated	$1,600.00	$1,600.00	$0.00	$0.00	$1,6
14	Final cleanup	$200.00	Prorated	$2,600.00	$2,400.00	$200.00	$0.00	$2,6
15	⊟ Print the book	$0.00	Prorated	$5,600.00	$5,600.00	$0.00	$0.00	$5,6
16	Prepare the files for desktop publishing	$0.00	Prorated	$1,400.00	$1,400.00	$0.00	$0.00	$1,4
17	Print the book	$0.00	Prorated	$4,200.00	$4,200.00	$0.00	$0.00	$4,2

Figure 7-16   The updated Cost table.

Reviewing Actual Project Costs

Once you've recorded actual project costs, you can view your actual costs in several useful ways using Project's Cost reports. For example, you can compare actual costs with budgeted costs.

To view Project's cost reports, take the following actions:

1. Choose the View menu's Reports command.

Project displays the Reports dialog box, as shown in Figure 7-17.

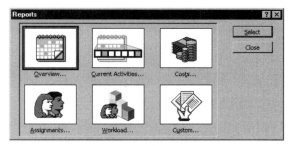

Figure 7-17   The Reports dialog box.

2. Choose the Costs category.

To do this, click Costs and then click the Select button. Project displays the Cost Reports dialog box, as shown in Figure 7-18.

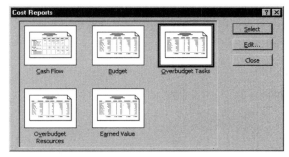

Figure 7-18   The Cost Reports dialog box.

3. Select a cost report.

To see a report, click it, and then click the Select button. Project produces an on-screen version of the report. Figure 7-19, for example, shows an Overbudget Tasks report, which lists tasks that show higher actual costs than budgeted costs.

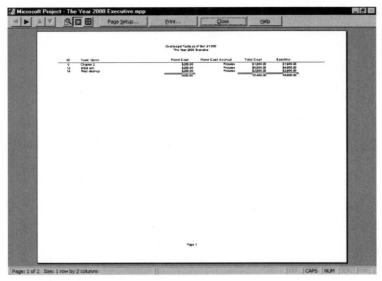

Figure 7-19   The Overbudget Tasks report in a Print Preview window.

Comparing Your Progress with Your Plan

After you've recorded some actual dates and costs, you can review your progress using still other tools in Project.

Using the Tracking Gantt View

If you want to take a look at the status of the tasks in your project in relationship to the baseline, use the Tracking Gantt view, as shown in Figure 7-20. This view gives you a visual picture of your project's progress. To display your project in Tracking Gantt view, click the Tracking Gantt icon on the View Bar.

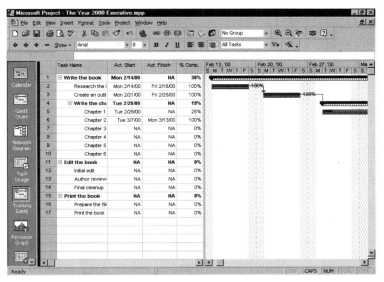

Figure 7-20 A picture of your project's progress in Tracking Gantt view.

Completed tasks or completed portions of tasks appear in dark blue on the chart, and the chart is labeled with percentages.

Using the Work Table

A Work table shows how many person hours are required to complete a task. Work is different from duration, which measures the total time allotted to the task. For example, if the duration of a task is one day, but the total work for the task is 16 hours, you'll need to add resources or extend the duration.

You can use the Work table to show the total time needed from all resources to complete the task. You can display a Work table for tasks and a Work table for resources. In both cases, the table displays baseline information so that you can compare actual to planned progress. To display a Work table for tasks, take the following actions:

1. **Open your project in Gantt Chart view.**

2. **Right-click the Select All button, and choose the shortcut menu's More Tables command.**

   Project displays the More Tables dialog box.

3. **Click Task.**

   Select Work from the list.

4. Click the Apply button.

Figure 7-21 shows the Work table for the tasks in the book-publishing project.

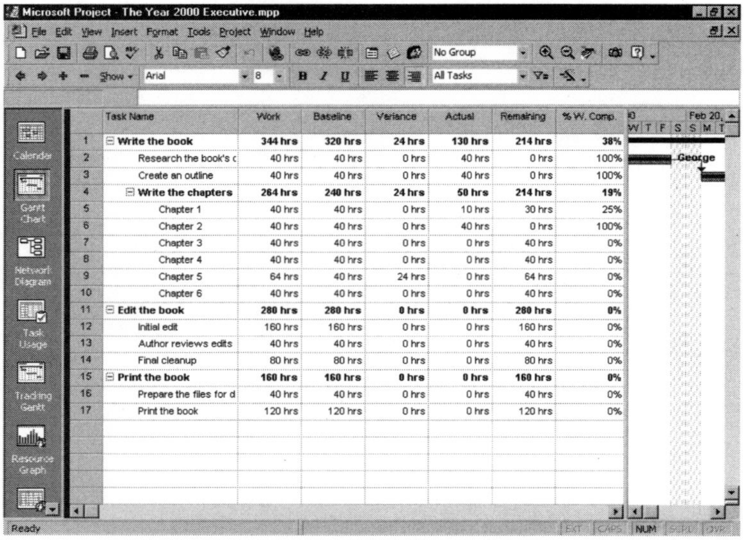

	Task Name	Work	Baseline	Variance	Actual	Remaining	% W. Comp.
1	Write the book	344 hrs	320 hrs	24 hrs	130 hrs	214 hrs	38%
2	Research the book's c	40 hrs	40 hrs	0 hrs	40 hrs	0 hrs	100%
3	Create an outline	40 hrs	40 hrs	0 hrs	40 hrs	0 hrs	100%
4	Write the chapters	264 hrs	240 hrs	24 hrs	50 hrs	214 hrs	19%
5	Chapter 1	40 hrs	40 hrs	0 hrs	10 hrs	30 hrs	25%
6	Chapter 2	40 hrs	40 hrs	0 hrs	40 hrs	0 hrs	100%
7	Chapter 3	40 hrs	40 hrs	0 hrs	0 hrs	40 hrs	0%
8	Chapter 4	40 hrs	40 hrs	0 hrs	0 hrs	40 hrs	0%
9	Chapter 5	64 hrs	40 hrs	24 hrs	0 hrs	64 hrs	0%
10	Chapter 6	40 hrs	40 hrs	0 hrs	0 hrs	40 hrs	0%
11	Edit the book	280 hrs	280 hrs	0 hrs	0 hrs	280 hrs	0%
12	Initial edit	160 hrs	160 hrs	0 hrs	0 hrs	160 hrs	0%
13	Author reviews edits	40 hrs	40 hrs	0 hrs	0 hrs	40 hrs	0%
14	Final cleanup	80 hrs	80 hrs	0 hrs	0 hrs	80 hrs	0%
15	Print the book	160 hrs	160 hrs	0 hrs	0 hrs	160 hrs	0%
16	Prepare the files for d	40 hrs	40 hrs	0 hrs	0 hrs	40 hrs	0%
17	Print the book	120 hrs	120 hrs	0 hrs	0 hrs	120 hrs	0%

Figure 7-21 A project open in Work table view for tasks.

To display a Work table for resources, take the following actions:

1. Open your project in Resource Usage view.

To do this, click the Resource Usage icon on the View Bar.

2. Right-click the Select All button, and choose the shortcut menu's Work command.

Figure 7-22 shows the book-publishing project open in a Work table for resources.

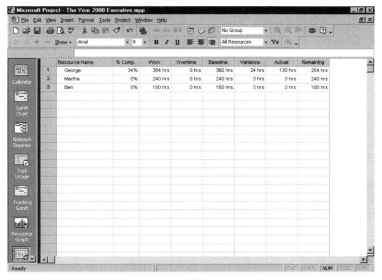

Figure 7-22   A project open in Work table view for resources.

Using Progress Lines

If you have saved a baseline with your project, you can add progress lines to the Gantt chart to connect in-progress tasks. To add a progress line, take the following actions:

1. **Open your project in Gantt Chart view.**

2. **Choose the Tools menu's Tracking command, and then select Progress Lines.**

    Project displays the Progress Lines dialog box, as shown in Figure 7-23.

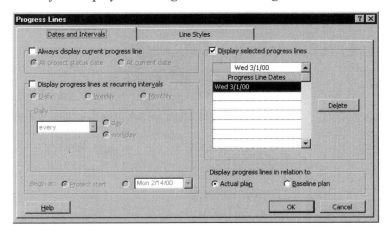

Figure 7-23   The Progress Lines dialog box.

3. If necessary, click the Dates And Intervals tab.

4. Specify the dates on which to show progress lines.

Select the Display Selected Progress Lines check box, and click Progress Line Dates to display a drop-down calendar.

5. Select a date.

6. Select either Actual Plan or Baseline Plan, and click OK.

Project displays a progress line in the Gantt chart similar to that in Figure 7-24.

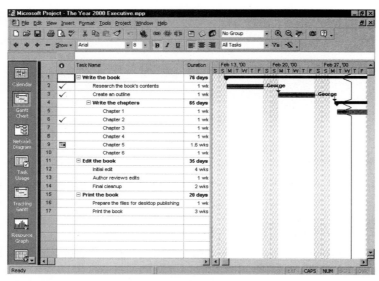

Figure 7-24   A progress line displayed in a Gantt chart.

Performing Earned Value Analysis

If you use Project to estimate and record costs and to track progress and you save project baseline information, you can also perform earned value analysis. In a nutshell, earned value analysis compares the percentages of work completed with the percentages of costs incurred. Table 7-1 summarizes the information that earned value analysis provides.

VALUE	DESCRIPTION
BCWS	An abbreviation for the Budgeted Cost of Work Scheduled. This amount shows the planned value of the work originally scheduled.
BCWP	An abbreviation for Budgeted Cost of Work Performed. This amount shows the planned value of the work completed.
ACWP	An abbreviation for Actual Cost of Work Performed. This amount shows the actual value, or cost, of the work completed.
SV	An abbreviation for Schedule Variance. This amount shows the difference between the BCWS and the BCWP.
CV	An abbreviation for Cost Variance. This amount shows the difference between BCWP and ACWP.
EAC	An abbreviation for Estimated At Completion. This amount shows the total actual cost incurred to date plus the remaining planned costs.
BAC	An abbreviation for Budgeted At Completion. This amount shows the total planned cost.
VAC	An abbreviation for Variance At Completion. This amount shows the difference between the BAC and the EAC.

Table 7-1   Amounts reported by earned value analysis.

NOTE   *"Step 1: Learn the Language" describes what earned value analysis is and how it works.*

Viewing the Earned Value Tables

You can view earned value analysis information for resources and for tasks. To view an earned value table for resources, take the following actions:

1. **Display the Resource Sheet.**

   You can do this by clicking the Resource Sheet icon on the View Bar.

2. **Tell Project you want to view the earned value table for resources.**

   You can do this by right-clicking the Select All button and choosing the shortcut menu's More Tables command. Then when Project displays the More Tables dialog box, click Earned Value and then click the Apply button. Project then displays the Earned Value table for resources, as shown in Figure 7-25.

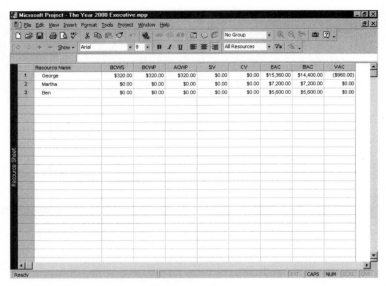

Figure 7-25   The Earned Value table for resources.

To view an Earned Value table for tasks, take the following actions:

1. Display the Task Sheet.

You can do this by displaying the Gantt Chart view or one of the other task views. To display the Gantt Chart view, click the Gantt Chart icon on the View Bar.

2. Tell Project you want to view the earned value table for tasks.

You can do this by right-clicking the Select All button and choosing the shortcut menu's More Tables command. Then when Project displays the More Tables dialog box, click Earned Value and click the Apply button. Project then displays the Earned Value table for tasks, as shown in Figure 7-26.

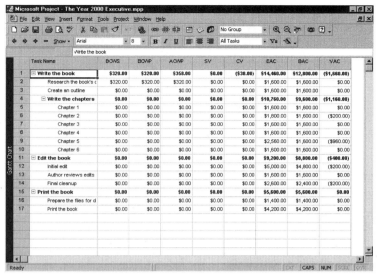

Figure 7-26 The Earned Value table for tasks.

Viewing an Earned Value Report

One of the other tools that Project provides for reviewing earned value analysis information is to the Earned Value report. To view the Earned Value report, take the following actions:

1. Choose the View menu's Reports command.

Project displays the Reports dialog box.

2. Choose the Costs category.

To do this, click Costs and then click the Select button. Project displays the Cost Reports dialog box.

3. Select the Earned Value report.

Click Earned Value, and then click the Select button. Project produces an on-screen version of the report.

Figure 7-27, for example, shows an Earned Value report.

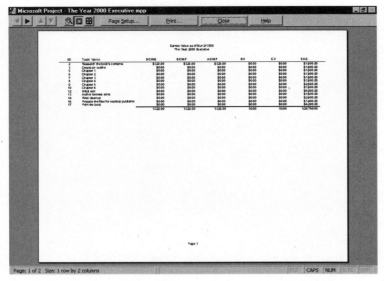

Figure 7-27 The Earned Value report in the Print Preview window.

Summary

This step looked at the many ways you can monitor the progress of your project in Project. One thing it didn't mention, however, is how you acquire the information you record in the various tables and dialog boxes. If your organization is sizable and you are not on a local area network, an intranet, or the Internet, getting the information you need may require some legwork or a procedure that ensures that you get regular status reports from those working on the project. The next step, "Step 8: Communicate Project Status," looks at how you can use workgroups and a network. Working over a network can simplify the job of collecting update information, although you'll still have to enter it in Project.

COMMUNICATE PROJECT STATUS

Tasks Required to Complete the Step

- Communicating via e-mail
- Using Project's web-based workgroup features

As you complete a project, you need to keep the team members apprised of the task status. Although traditional means of communication (face-to-face meetings, telephone calls, letters) may work well for some tasks, other times you might want to immediately communicate detailed information about a project to people in diverse areas. To facilitate doing so, Microsoft Project 2000 has built-in Internet features allowing you to quickly and easily send e-mail regarding project status or post a Project file on the World Wide Web so that people in different locations can access and edit it as necessary.

Communicating via E-Mail

Project provides several ways with which you can use e-mail to communicate about a project. As do most Microsoft programs, Project allows you to send a file in various formats. Project also allows you to send special e-mail task requests, task updates, and status reports.

Regardless of which e-mail functions you decide to use with Project, it helps to display the Workgroup toolbar. To do so, choose the View menu's Toolbars command and choose the submenu's Workgroup command. Figure 8-1 shows the Workgroup toolbar.

Figure 8-1   The Workgroup toolbar.

Sending a Project File

To send a project file as an e-mail message attachment, click the Send To Mail Recipient (As Attachment) button on the Workgroup toolbar. Clicking this button displays a new message form in your default e-mail client. Address and complete the message in the usual way. Figure 8-2 shows a message filled out in Microsoft Outlook Express. In Outlook Express, you click the Send toolbar button to send the message.

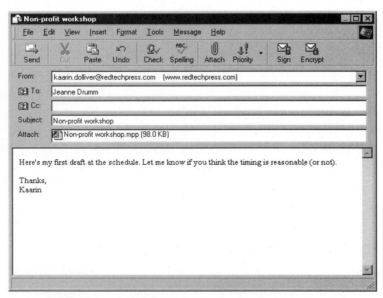

Figure 8-2   Sending a Project file as an e-mail attachment.

NOTE *If you send a Project 2000 file as an attachment, the message recipient must have Project 2000 to be able to read the file. If the recipient doesn't have this version, you need to save the file in a different format and then attach the file to a new message from your e-mail client.*

Click the Send To Routing Recipient toolbar button to open the Routing Slip dialog box shown in Figure 8-3.

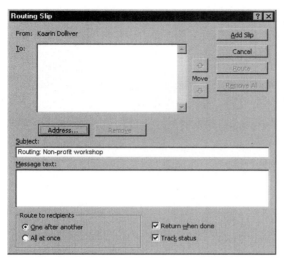

Figure 8-3   The Routing Slip dialog box.

Click the Address button to select recipients from your address book. After you have selected the recipients, use the Routing Slip dialog box's Move buttons to move recipients up and down in the route. Click the Route button to route the messages. Click the Add Slip button to add the routing slip to the project and close the Routing Slip dialog box.

After the first routing recipient opens the file and saves any changes, he or she chooses the File menu's Send To command and then chooses the submenu's Next Routing Recipient command to send the file to the next recipient on the list.

If you work on a network with a Microsoft Exchange server, you can post a Project file to a public folder by clicking the Send To Exchange Folder toolbar button.

NOTE   *To post to an Exchange folder, you need to have an e-mail client capable of working with the Microsoft Exchange Server service (such as Outlook) installed as your default e-mail client.*

Using an E-Mail-Based Workgroup

To communicate about a project file via a network e-mail system, you first need to make sure that all of the workgroup members (the resources involved in the project), have a MAPI-compliant, 32-bit e-mail client, such as Outlook or Exchange.

Then you need to make sure that any team members who don't have Project installed on their computers run the file WGSETUP.EXE, which is located on the Project CD-ROM. This sets up the Workgroup Message Handler.

Setting Up the Project for an E-Mail-Based Workgroup

After you have completed the preliminary steps, you're ready to set up the Project file for using e-mail. To do this, you first need to make sure that you have all of the workgroup members' e-mail addresses stored in your address book. To do so, take the following actions:

1. **Open the Project file containing the resources with whom you want to communicate via e-mail.**

   If you're using a resource pool across multiple projects, open the resource pool.

   NOTE *"Step 4: Identify and Allocate Resources" describes setting up and working with resource pools.*

2. **Display the Resource Sheet.**

   Click the Resource Sheet icon on the View Bar to display the Resource Sheet if you're not currently displaying it.

3. **Double-click the resource with whom you want to communicate via e-mail.**

   Project displays the General tab of the Resource Information dialog box, as shown in Figure 8-4.

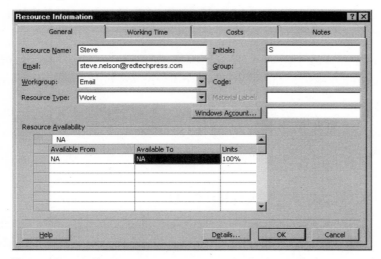

Figure 8-4   Setting up a resource to receive e-mail about a project.

4. Select Email from the Workgroup drop-down list box.

5. Click the Details button.

   If Project finds a contact in your address book that matches the resource's name, it displays the properties for that contact. If Project can't find a resource, it displays the Check Names dialog box, as shown in Figure 8-5.

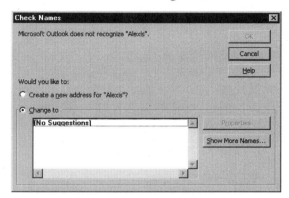

Figure 8-5   The Check Names dialog box.

NOTE   *If Project finds multiple entries that match the name you entered, it lists them in the Check Names dialog box. Select the correct entry, and click OK.*

- Click the Show More Names button if you believe that you have the resource's e-mail address in your address book. Project allows you to view the list of contacts in your address book and select the correct one.

- Click the Create A New Address option button to create a new contact entry.

Assigning Tasks or Projects over E-Mail

To assign a task or project to a workgroup member via e-mail and request a response, you use a TeamAssign message. The task request recipient can either accept or decline the request. If he or she doesn't reply, Project assumes that he or she has accepted the assignment. To create a TeamAssign message, take the following actions:

1. **Display in Gantt Chart view the project containing the tasks you want to assign.**

2. **If you want to assign only some tasks, select those tasks.**

3. **Click the TeamAssign toolbar button.**

If you selected a single task, Project displays the Workgroup Mail dialog box, as shown in Figure 8-6. Click the All Tasks option button to send a message assigning the entire project, or click the Selected Task option button to send a message assigning only the selected task. Click OK.

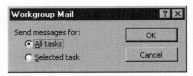

Figure 8-6   The Workgroup Mail dialog box.

4. **Complete the task assignment message.**

In the TeamAssign dialog box, as shown in Figure 8-7, enter a message subject and edit the message body text as necessary.

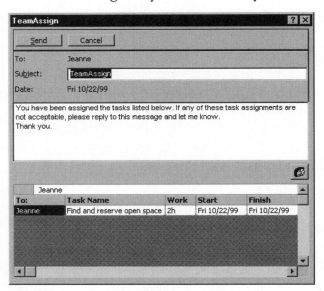

Figure 8-7   The TeamAssign dialog box.

If necessary, remove, replace, or add resources assigned to the task. Click the Assign Resources toolbar button. Project displays the Resource Assignment dialog box, as shown in Figure 8-8.

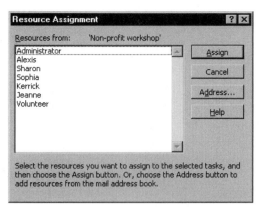

Figure 8-8   The Resource Assignment dialog box.

- Click Address to add resources from your address book.

- To add a resource from the current resource pool, select the resource's name from the Resources From list and click the Assign button.

- To remove a resource, select the resource's name from the Entry bar above the list of tasks and press the Delete key.

NOTE   *If you add or remove resources in the manner above, Project adds or removes them from the task assignment, not just from the list of recipients receiving the e-mail.*

5. **Click the Send button to send the message.**

   Project places the task assignment message in your Outbox. Depending on the services you use and how you have your e-mail client set up, you may need to deliver the message by clicking a button in your e-mail program or by making a dial-up connection to the Internet. Figure 8-9 shows how a task assignment message looks in Outlook.

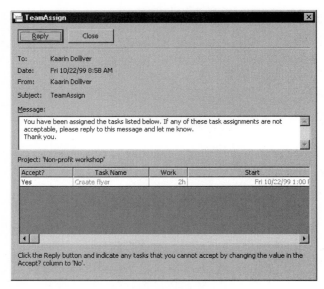

Figure 8-9   A task assignment e-mail message.

NOTE   *Project sends the file as an .MXM attachment.*

To reply to a task assignment message, open the message, click the Reply button, and leave the default of Yes in the Accept? box to accept the request or enter No in the Accept? box to decline the request. Then click the Send button. When you receive a reply to a task request, open the message and click Update Project to update the project.

Sending Task Updates over E-Mail

To inform a workgroup member of a change to a task to which the member is assigned, you use a TeamUpdate message. If you have sent out a task request for a task and received a response, and then later edit the task, Project alerts you that you need to update the team by placing an icon of an envelope and an exclamation point in the Indicator column of the Gantt chart. To send an update for the task, select the task and click the TeamUpdate toolbar button. To change the subject for the update, enter a new subject in the Subject box. To edit the message, enter text in the message area. Click the Send button to send the TeamUpdate message.

To reply to a TeamUpdate message you've received, first open the message and enter your reply in the message area. To accept the message without making any changes, click the Reply button. To update your record of the tasks to reflect the changes, click Update Task List.

Sending Status Reports over E-Mail

To request a progress report on a task, you use a TeamStatus message. The recipient can reply with status information, which you can incorporate into the project.

To send a TeamStatus message, select the task in question and click the TeamUpdate toolbar button. To change the subject for the message, enter a new subject in the Subject box. To edit the message, enter text in the message area. Click the Send button to send the TeamUpdate message.

To reply to a TeamStatus message you've received, open the message and click Reply. Then enter the requested information in the appropriate boxes and click Send to send the message immediately or Save And Send Later to postpone sending the message.

Using Project's Web-Based Workgroup Features

Project's web features allow workgroup members to communicate from a web browser to Microsoft Internet Information Server (IIS), which stores project information such as resource assignments in a database format. To use the web-based workgroup features in Project, you need to have a web server set up for publishing the Project information, and workgroup members must have either Internet Explorer 4.01 Service Pack 1 or later or they must install the Browser Module included with Project.

Setting Up a Web Server with Microsoft Project Central

If you don't have a web server with Microsoft Project Central installed, you need to set up the server. The web server must meet the following requirements:

- Windows NT Server 4.0 with Service Pack 4 or higher or Windows 2000 with Microsoft Internet Information Server (IIS) 4.0 or later

- If you are using Windows NT 4.0, Windows NT Option Pack 4.0 to install Internet Information Server (IIS) 4.0

- SQL Server 7.0, Oracle Server 8.0, or Microsoft Database Engine (MSDE, which is included on the Project CD-ROM)

NOTE *You can download a service pack or the option pack at* http://www.Microsoft.com/NTServer/all/downloads.asp.

To set up the web server, insert the Project CD-ROM and click Install Microsoft Project Central Server in the Microsoft Project 2000 Setup dialog box, as shown in Figure 8-10. If the Setup screen doesn't appear when you insert the CD, view the CD in Windows NT Explorer and double-click WEBSVR.MSI.

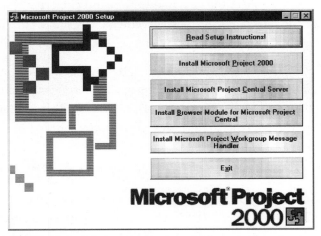

Figure 8-10   Installing Microsoft Project 2000 Server.

To continue with the installation procedure, take the following actions:

1. **Enter your user name and organization.**

   Click Next to proceed.

2. **Accept the terms of the license agreement.**

   Click the I Accept The Terms In The License Agreement option button, and click Next to proceed.

3. **Click the Install Now button.**

   This performs a typical installation, installing the standard components in the default locations.

4. **After the installation completes, restart the server if prompted to do so.**

Setting Up the Browser Module

If the members of the workgroup don't want to use Internet Explorer as their browser, they need to set up the Browser Module included with Project. To do so, take the following actions:

1. **Insert the Project CD-ROM, and click Install Browser Module for Microsoft Project Central.**

   If the Setup screen doesn't appear when you insert the CD, view the CD in Windows NT Explorer and double-click WEBCLNT.MSI.

   Follow the installation procedure, entering your user name, initials, and organization, accepting the terms of the license agreement, and clicking the Install Now button. After the installation completes, restart the computer if the setup program prompts you to do so.

2. **After the Browser Module is installed, run it.**

   Click the Start button, choose Programs, and click Browser Module For Microsoft Project Central.

3. **Choose the Tools menu's Server Settings command.**

   Project displays the Server Settings dialog box, as shown in Figure 8-11.

Figure 8-11   The Server Settings dialog box.

4. **Click the Add button to specify the web server.**

   Project displays the Add Server dialog box, as shown in Figure 8-12.

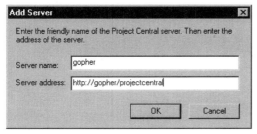

Figure 8-12   Adding a web server.

5. Describe the server.

Enter a friendly name for the server, and enter the server address in the format *http:/ /<server name>/projectcentral*. Then click OK twice.

NOTE *If you use a proxy server to access the web server, choose the Tools menu's Internet Options command, click the Connections tab, and click the LAN Settings button. Then enter the proxy information, and click OK.*

Figure 8-13 shows how the Browser Module looks after you have entered and connected to a Project web server.

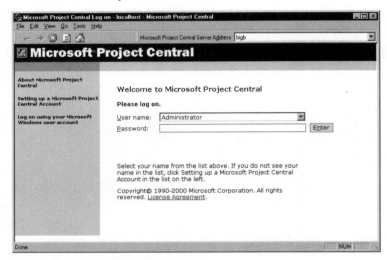

Figure 8-13 The Browser Module.

Setting Up a Workgroup in a Project

1. Choose the Tools menu's Options command, and click the Workgroup tab.

Project displays the Workgroup tab of the Options dialog box, as shown in Figure 8-14.

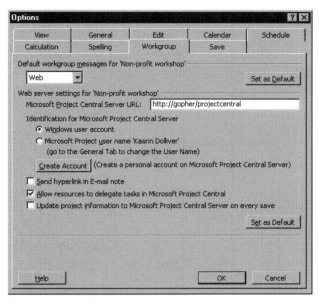

Figure 8-14   Setting up a workgroup in Project.

2. **Select Web from the Default Workgroup Messages For drop-down list box.**

3. **Enter the Project web server URL in the Microsoft Project Central Server URL box.**

   Enter the URL in the format *http://<server name>/projectcentral*.

4. **Specify how you want to log on to the server.**

   Click the Windows User Account option button to use your Windows account. Click the Microsoft Project User Name option button to use your Project user name as entered on the General tab of the Options dialog box, or click the Create Account button to create a new account on the Project Central Server.

   Select the Allow Resources To Delegate Tasks In Microsoft Project Central check box to allow resources to delegate tasks. Select the Update Project Information To Microsoft Project Central Server On Every Save check box if you want Project to update changes to the project automatically every time you save the file.

Using the Inbox

After you have set up a workgroup, click the TeamInbox toolbar button to log on to your account and see whether you have any messages, tasks, or status reports awaiting you. Internet Explorer (or the Browser Module) displays the Microsoft Project Central web site, as shown in Figure 8-15.

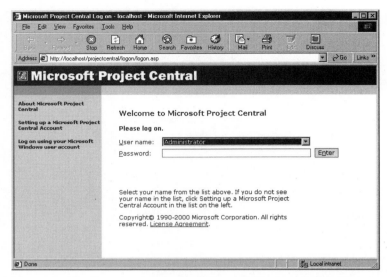

Figure 8-15　Logging on to the Microsoft Project Central Server.

Enter your password, and click the Enter button.

The browser displays any messages, tasks, or status reports, as shown in Figure 8-16.

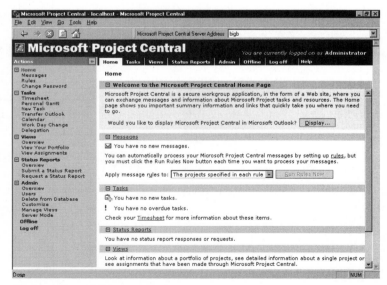

Figure 8-16　The Project Central home page.

You navigate through Project Central by clicking hyperlinks in the Actions pane on the left side or by resting the mouse pointer over the tabs along the bar at the top and choosing areas from the drop-down menus that appear.

To log off Project Central, click the Log Off hyperlink in the Actions pane.

Reading Messages

To read your messages, click the Microsoft Project Central Inbox hyperlink. Figure 8-17 shows the Inbox.

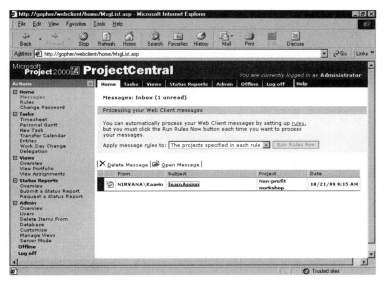

Figure 8-17   The Inbox.

To read a message, click its hyperlink. Figure 8-18 shows a message for an automatically accepted task. To decline a task request, click the Reply button, click the Accept? column for the task, and select No from the drop-down list box. Optionally, enter a comment in the Comment column. Then click the Send button.

NOTE   *You can make changes only to the white Accept? and Comment columns for tasks. You cannot make changes to any grayed-out summary tasks to which these tasks belong.*

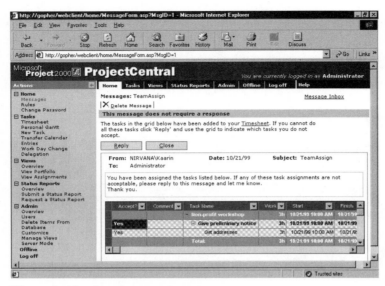

Figure 8-18 A task request message.

Creating Message Rules

To set up message rules, click the Rules hyperlink under the Home heading in the Actions pane and click the New Rule button. This starts the Rules Wizard, as shown in Figure 8-19.

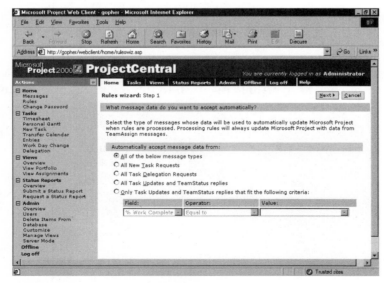

Figure 8-19 Creating message rules.

Proceed through the steps of the wizard by specifying the rules you want to create and clicking Next after each step of the wizard.

Viewing Personal Timesheets

To view a personal timesheet of the tasks to which you've been assigned, click the Timesheet hyperlink under the Tasks heading in the Actions pane. Figure 8-20 shows a timesheet listing three tasks. The timesheet describes the tasks in the left pane and displays a calendar in the right pane.

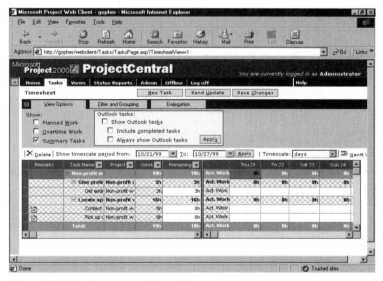

Figure 8-20 A personal timesheet.

By default, the timesheet lists the tasks to which you've been assigned for all projects. If you want to view tasks for selected projects, click the drop-down arrow in the Project column and select a specific project or select Custom to specify multiple projects.

To change the date range for the tasks you view in the timesheet, enter different values in the Show Timescale Period From boxes.

To enter work you've completed, enter values in the white boxes of the Remaining and % Work Complete columns, and, optionally, enter comments in the Comments column. Then click the Send Update button to update the project manager.

Viewing Personal Gantt Charts

A personal Gantt chart provides another way for you to view the tasks to which you've been assigned. To display a personal Gantt chart, click the Personal Gantt hyperlink under the Tasks heading in the Actions pane. The Project Central personal Gantt chart looks much like the Gantt chart in Project, except that it displays tasks for the logged-on workgroup member only. Figure 8-21 shows a personal Gantt chart.

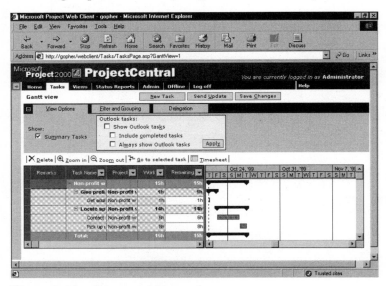

Figure 8-21   A personal Gantt chart.

As with the timesheet, you can create and send task updates from the personal Gantt chart. Just enter values in the white boxes of the Remaining and % Work Complete columns, and, optionally, enter comments in the Comments column. Then click the Send Update button to update the project manager.

NOTE   *You can send task update information to a recipient's Project Central Inbox from Project by clicking the TeamUpdate button on the Workgroup toolbar, as described earlier in this step.*

To delegate a task, click the Delegation tab. Then select the task, and click the Delegate Task button. In the two-step delegation process, specify the workgroup member to whom you want to delegate the task, whether you want to assume the lead role for the task or pass on the management of the task to the project manager, and whether you want to continue tracking the task.

NOTE   *You can send a task assignment to a recipient's Project Central Inbox from Project by clicking the TeamAssign toolbar button on the Workgroup toolbar, as described earlier in this step.*

Creating New Tasks

To create a new task, click the New Task hyperlink under the Tasks heading in the Actions pane. The browser displays the page shown in Figure 8-22.

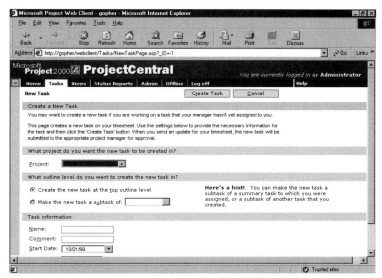

Figure 8-22   Adding a new task.

Requesting Status Reports

To request a status report, click the Request A Status Report hyperlink under the Status Reports heading in the Actions pane. Then click the Create, Edit, Or Delete hyperlink in the Actions pane. Specify whether you want to set up, edit, or delete a status report, and click OK. Project Central displays step 1 of the four steps for creating a status report, as shown in Figure 8-23.

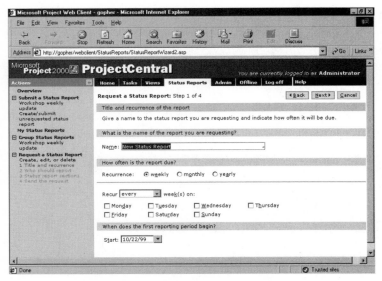

Figure 8-23   Creating a status report.

In the first step, name the report and describe when it should occur. In the second step, specify the resources who should respond to the report. In the third step, indicate the topics on which you want the workgroup members to send status information. In the fourth step, save the status report or send it immediately. Project Central lists status report responses you've received on the home page under the New Status Reports Received heading in the Status Reports section. Click the report's hyperlink to read it.

NOTE   *You can send a status report to a recipient's Project Central Inbox from Project by clicking the TeamStatus toolbar button on the Workgroup toolbar, as described earlier in this step.*

Responding to Status Reports

To respond to a status report, click the status report's hyperlink on the home page. Project Central displays the status report, as shown in Figure 8-24.

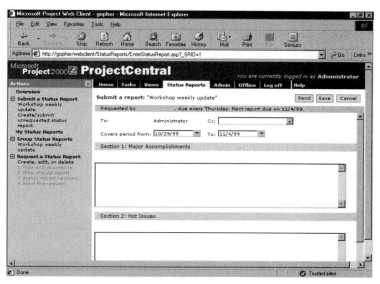

Figure 8-24 Filling out a status report.

To copy someone else on the status report, select that resource from the Cc: drop-down list box. Enter the requested information in the list boxes provided or click the Insert Tasks From Timesheet button to display a list of scheduled tasks, then select Yes in the Insert column for the tasks you want to insert, click Insert Tasks, and click Done when you've finished inserting the tasks. To add information to the status report, click the Click Here To Add Another Section button. When you've completed the status report, click the Send button.

NOTE   *To add, modify, delete, or merge user accounts and to customize Project Central settings, click the Users hyperlink under the Admin heading in the Actions pane.*

Summary

In this step we looked at the ways you can use e-mail and Project Central to communicate project status with workgroup members. This is the final activity of creating a project. In the appendixes of this book we describe how to use Network Diagrams to deal with scheduling uncertainties, how to use Project's tools for working with complex projects, how to link multiple projects, and how to customize Project to suit your needs.

Appendix A

SCHEDULE PROJECT UNCERTAINTIES

In This Appendix

- Understanding PERT analysis
- The PERT way to estimate
- Working with a Network Diagram (PERT chart)

In Step 1, we looked briefly at PERT analysis and showed you a diagram of how a project looks in a PERT chart. We also mentioned that in Microsoft Project 2000 a PERT chart is called a Network Diagram, and in Step 5 we looked at a project in Network Diagram view. In this appendix, we want to give you some background information about PERT, and then we'll show you in detail how you can use Project and PERT to do what-if analysis.

In plain English, what-if analysis, or PERT analysis, involves estimating how your project will go under the best of circumstances, under the expected circumstances, and under the worst of circumstances. As we've mentioned, one reason for using Project is to make a plan and then review it in order to avoid surprises. If you do some what-if analysis early in your project, you may be able to change your plan so that you're prepared for the worst of circumstances, or, at the very least, you won't be surprised when your worst nightmare comes true.

Understanding PERT Analysis

When you are scheduling a project, you can base it on information you've developed in a couple of ways:

- With information you've gathered about past experience
- With estimates

Suppose, for example, that each year you produce an annual report. You have a good idea, based on how things went in previous years, of how long it will take to prepare the financials, get the letter from the CEO, prepare the introductory text, shoot and lay out the photos, run everything through legal, and so on. If you used Project to manage this project, you even have documentation of the actuals. As you input tasks and durations, you can use historical data. (You might even use the previous year's file as a template.)

What do you do, however, if you have no past experience with most of the tasks in a project? You make your best guess based on whatever relevant experience you have. In other words, you estimate. The element of risk associated with your estimate is probably in direct proportion to the uniqueness of the task. For example, if you're preparing an annual report for the first time and you've never dealt with desktop publishing, the production process, or the printing process, the risk that you'll under-estimate the time you need for these tasks is high, which means that the project will get out of control.

Are you doomed? Not necessarily. You need a way to reduce the risk of estimating, and this is where PERT comes in. PERT was developed about 1958 in response to this problem. Originally applied to the Polaris submarine project, PERT was a joint effort of the U.S. Navy and the consulting firm of Booz, Allen, and Hamilton. PERT is based on the notion that estimates are uncertain and that it is reasonable to use ranges of duration and then determine the probability that a task will fall into a range.

The PERT Way to Estimate

Even if you have no direct experience with most of the tasks in a project, in most cases you have relevant experience and can make an educated guess about the *most likely* duration of a task. You can probably also make educated guesses about how long a task will take in the best and worse circumstances. In other words, you can envision *pessimistic* and *optimistic* scenarios. In PERT analysis, all three situations are defined precisely:

- In an *optimistic* scenario, the time would be improved only 1 time in 20 if the task could be completed repeatedly under the same essential conditions.

- In a *most likely* scenario, the duration of a task is the time that is most likely to occur more often than any other.

- In a *pessimistic* scenario, the time would be exceeded only 1 time in 20 if the activity could be performed repeatedly under the same essential conditions.

You can think of these three scenarios as representations of aspects of the normal distribution curve that you could draw if the task were performed a sufficient number of times. And if all this is beginning to sound like statistics to you, you're right. But you don't have to do the calculations; Project does them for you.

Working with a Network Diagram (PERT Chart)

PERT analysis deals with duration, whereas PERT charts, also called Network Diagrams, deal with relationships. A Network Diagram view is your project graphically represented as a flowchart. Figure A-1 shows a simple project in Network Diagram view. To open a project in Network Diagram view, click the Network Diagram icon on the View Bar or choose the View menu's Network Diagram command.

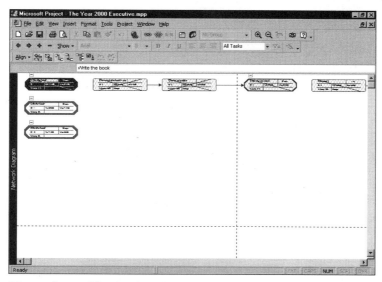

Figure A-1   The book-publishing project in Network Diagram view.

NOTE   *If you upgraded from Project 2000, you may have a PERT icon on the View Bar instead of a Network Diagram icon.*

In Network Diagram view, each box, also called a *node,* represents a single task. Predecessors are above successors, and summary tasks are above subtasks. Two diagonal lines through a box indicate that the task is completed; a single diagonal line indicates that a task is partially completed. If a box has no diagonal line, the task has not begun. Red lines represent critical path relationships, and black lines represent noncritical path relationships.

To display more or less of the Network Diagram, click the Zoom In and Zoom Out toolbar buttons.

To see how other aspects of a project are displayed in Network Diagram view and to edit the display, double-click anywhere in a blank area of a Network Diagram to open the Box Styles dialog box, as shown in Figure A-2. Click an item in the Style Settings For list to display a preview of it in the Preview box. Use the drop-down list boxes in the lower half of the Box Styles dialog box to change symbols and colors associated with boxes (nodes).

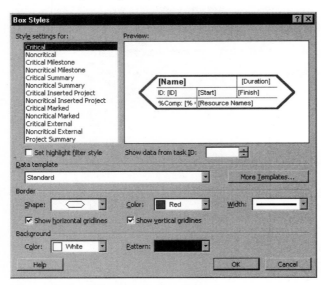

Figure A-2   The Box Styles dialog box.

To change the view of the Network Diagram, you use the buttons on the Network Diagram toolbar, which is shown in Figure A-3. In left-to-right order, the buttons are as follows:

• Align

- Show Summary Tasks
- Show Progress Marks
- Show Page Breaks
- Show Link Labels
- Straight Links
- Hide Fields
- Layout Now
- Layout Selection Now

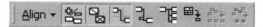

Figure A-3   The Network Diagram toolbar.

If you want to rearrange the layout of the Network Diagram, you use the options in the Layout dialog box, as shown in Figure A-4. To open this dialog box, choose the Format menu's Layout command or right-click an empty area of the diagram and choose the shortcut menu's Layout command.

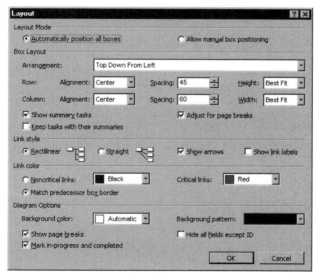

Figure A-4   The Layout dialog box.

Use the options in the Layout dialog box to change the layout mode (your choices are automatic and manual), the layout of boxes, the link style and color, the background color and pattern, and the page breaks.

Appendix B

DEAL WITH PROJECT COMPLEXITY

In This Appendix

- Simplifying dependency relationships
- Dividing a large project into multiple subprojects
- Using WBS codes
- Using macros to automate actions

The simple approach described in the steps of this book works for most projects. In our own experiences, such a "keep it simple" approach works well even when projects become more complex because the number of tasks, dependences, constraints, and resources grow.

In a certain number of cases, unfortunately, you will need to complicate your project plans to deal with the realities of a project. This appendix describes some of the tools that Microsoft Project 2000 supplies for recognizing and dealing with these real-world complexities.

Simplifying Dependency Relationships

You can often avoid the sort of fine-tuning of task durations described in Step 3 by working with complete and detailed sets of tasks. This is especially true if you begin to use lag time in your relationships. Lag time often indicates that you're either working with incomplete detail in your tasks or missing tasks.

In some cases, when you work with dependency relationships other than the standard finish-to-start relationship and include lag time, it's because one of the tasks in the relationship is really a summary task. And what you're doing is trying to show that one part of the predecessor task needs to finish before the successor task or one part of the successor task can start.

Take the case of a book manuscript, for example. You might say at first blush that the book manuscript needs to be written before it can be edited. And then, when confronted with the need to compress the schedule in order to meet some deadline, you might say that, well, you can actually start editing while the writer is still writing.

Given the scenario described in the preceding paragraph, you might decide that rather than working with a standard finish-to-start dependency relationship, you can work with a start-to-start dependency relationship as long as the start of the successor task lags the start of the predecessor by, say, one week.

Often, however, a better way to deal with this reality—the reality that the editor can start working before the writer is finished writing—is to break the writing and editing tasks into smaller subtasks. A Write Manuscript task might be broken into two subtasks: Write Chapters 1 to 5 and Write Chapters 6 to 10. An Edit Manuscript task might similarly be broken into two subtasks: Edit Chapters 1 to 5 and Edit Chapters 6 to 10.

Once the project schedule more closely matches reality, it's easy to work with simple finish-to-start dependency relationships and zero lag times. The Write Chapters 1 to 5 task needs to finish before the Edit Chapters 1 to 5 task can start. The Write Chapters 6 to 10 task needs to finish before the Edit Chapters 6 to 10 task can start. In both dependencies, the relationship is finish-to-start and the lag time equals zero.

Lag times may also indicate that a project schedule is simply missing a task. For example, suppose you're working with a two-task project for painting some interior office space. The first and predecessor task might be Paint Office. The second and successor task might be Clean Up. In this scenario, you might use a lag time equal to the time required for the paint to dry.

Another option—often preferable because it's simpler—is to create a task for Let paint dry. In this case, you then work with three tasks, all with finish-to-start dependency relationships, and all with zero lag-time settings. What's more, replacing the lag time with an actual task, Let Paint Dry, explains and highlights the lag time.

We recommend you adopt the strategy of working with detailed task lists as a way to minimize the sort of complexity that comes from dependency fine-tuning. If you do adopt such a strategy, however, you end up with voluminous numbers of project tasks. To deal with this drawback, you probably want to use summary tasks in your schedules. Using summary tasks will make it easy to present project schedule information in a summarized fashion—something that will probably make project management and project reporting easier.

NOTE   *"Step 3: Schedule Project Tasks" explains how to create and use summary tasks.*

Dividing a Large Project into Multiple Subprojects

If you have a complex project with many tasks, you can create subprojects and save them as separate files to work with them independently and focus on one area at a time. To create subprojects from a large project, take the following actions:

1. **Display the large Project file in Gantt Chart view.**

   To do this, open the project and click the Gantt Chart icon on the View Bar.

2. **Select the tasks you want to save in the first subproject file, and click the Copy toolbar button.**

   Project copies the tasks you selected to the Clipboard.

3. **Click the New toolbar button to create a new file.**

   Project displays the Project Information dialog box, as shown in Figure B-1.

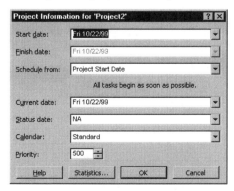

Figure B-1   The Project Information dialog box.

4. Enter the Project start and finish dates and the scheduling method. Verify the current date, and select a calendar to use for the project.

5. Click the Paste toolbar button.

6. Save the subproject.

7. Redisplay the large project file.

Repeat the procedure for subsequent subproject files.

NOTE   *"Appendix C: Work with Multiple Projects" describes how you can link tasks across separate project files. "Step 4: Identify and Allocate Resources" describes how you can share a resource pool among multiple project files.*

Using WBS Codes

It often helps to outline complex projects using a system called Work Breakdown Structure, or WBS. WBS codes number tasks according to their position in the outline. For example, if your project is landscaping your yard, the tasks might be as follows:

1. Cut down trees.

2. Remove tree stumps.

3. Grade lot.

4. Remove poor soil.

5. Install underground irrigation system.

6. Spread sand.

7. Lay sod.

8. Plant mounds.

The WBS code for the first task is just 1. If this first task includes the following subtasks:

1. Obtain permit for tree removal.

2. Have power lines lowered.

3. Climb trees.

4. Clear brush.

these tasks would have the WBS codes 1.1, 1.2, 1.3, and 1.4 respectively. And if the first task contained the subtasks:

1. Go to city for information and forms.

2. Sketch plans.

3. Fill out form.

4. Write check.

these tasks would have the WBS codes 1.1.1, 1.1.2, and 1.1.3 respectively. To display WBS codes in Project, take the following actions:

1. **Choose the Tools menu's Options command, and click the View tab.**

   Project displays the Options dialog box, as shown in Figure B-2.

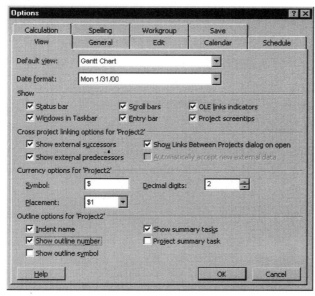

Figure B-2   The View tab of the Options dialog box.

2. **Select the Show Outline Number check box, and click OK.**

   Figure B-3 shows how the project in the above example looks with WBS codes displayed.

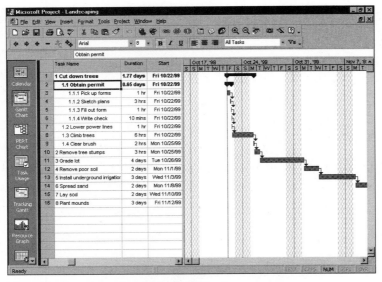

Figure B-3   A project with WBS codes.

To insert a column for the WBS codes, choose the Insert menu's Column command. In the Column Definition dialog box, select WBS from the Field Name drop-down list box and click OK.

If your company uses customized WBS codes for project management, you can define these codes in Project. To do so, choose the Project menu's WBS command and choose the submenu's Define Code command. Project displays the WBS Code Definition dialog box for the current project, as shown in Figure B-4. Use this dialog box to specify the code mask for each level.

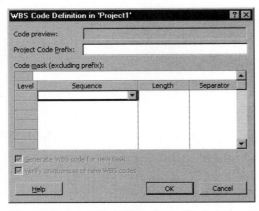

Figure B-4   The WBS Code Definition dialog box.

WBS codes work much like the outline codes described in "Step 7: Manage Project Progress," except outline codes do not necessarily match the outline structure of your project, as do WBS codes. For example, you can create outline codes based on your company's cost codes. For more information about outline codes and specifying code masks, see Step 7.

Using Macros to Automate Actions

You can speed your work in complex projects by using macros to automate repetitive tasks. If you have programming experience, you can write your macro in Microsoft Visual Basic for Applications. You can also create a program by recording a series of actions into a macro.

NOTE *To program in Visual Basic for Applications, choose the Tools menu's Macro command and choose the submenu's Visual Basic Editor command.*

To record a macro, take the following actions:

1. **Plan and practice the actions you want to record.**

   Go through the actions, and, if necessary, take notes to remember the order of actions you want to record.

2. **Choose the Tools menu's Macro command, and choose the submenu's Record New Macro command.**

   Project displays the Record Macro dialog box, as shown in Figure B-5.

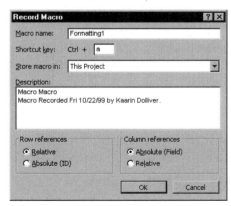

Figure B-5   The Record Macro dialog box.

3. **Name the macro.**

The macro name must begin with a letter and not a number or other character. Macro names cannot contain spaces.

4. **Optionally, assign a keyboard shortcut to the macro.**

Enter a letter in the Shortcut Key box. If you select a letter that Project already uses to perform an action, Project displays a warning and requires that you choose a different letter. For example, the Ctrl+S combination is the keyboard shortcut for saving. If you enter S in the dialog box, Project displays a warning when you click OK.

5. **Specify the storage location for the macro.**

To make a macro available to all projects, select Global File from the Store Macro In drop-down list box. To make the macro available in only the current project, select This Project from the Store Macro In drop-down list box.

NOTE *If you store a macro in the current project and later want to copy the macro to a template for use in other projects, you can use Project's Organizer feature. Choose the Tools menu's Organizer command, and click the Modules tab.*

6. **Describe the macro.**

7. **Specify how the macro should select rows and columns.**

   - Click the Relative option button in the Row References section if you want the macro to begin with the selected cell when it is run.

   - Click the Absolute (ID) option button if you want the macro to always begin in the same row, regardless of which cell is selected when the macro is run.

   - Click the Absolute (Field) option button in the Column References section if you want the macro to always begin in the same row, regardless of which cell is selected when the macro is run.

   - Click the Relative option button if you want the macro to begin with the selected cell.

8. **Click OK.**

Project begins recording your actions.

TIP *Project does not record the pace of your actions, so time is not of the essence. Take your time to complete the actions carefully rather than hurrying and needing to record the macro again.*

9. **When you're finished, choose the Tools menu's Macro command and choose the submenu's Stop Recorder command.**

Project stops recording your macro and saves the macro in the location you specified.

To run the macro, choose the Tools menu's Macro command and choose the submenu's Macros command to open the dialog box shown in Figure B-6.

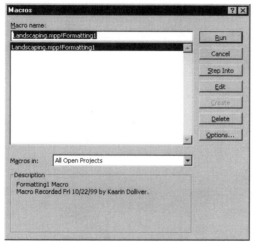

Figure B-6 The Macros dialog box.

Select the macro you want to run from the Macro Name list, and click the Run button. Project performs the actions you recorded.

TIP *If you assigned a keyboard shortcut to the macro, you can quickly run the macro by pressing the shortcut key. You can also create a custom toolbar button for a macro. For more information about creating custom toolbar buttons, see "Appendix D: Customize Project."*

Appendix C

WORK WITH MULTIPLE PROJECTS

In This Appendix

- Creating a consolidated project file for multiple projects
- Updating links of source projects
- Linking tasks across separate project files

If you manage more than one project at a single time, chances are high that the projects interact in some way. Perhaps a task in one project depends on a task in another. Or perhaps resources require leveling across all projects. Luckily, Microsoft Project 2000 allows you to consolidate multiple projects into one large file so you can work with numerous projects together.

NOTE   *The same feature that allows you to consolidate multiple projects also lets you divide a large project into more manageable subprojects and work with the subprojects individually.*

Creating a Consolidated Project File for Multiple Projects

To consolidate Project files into one large Project file with multiple subprojects, take the following actions:

1. Create a new project file for the consolidated project.

NOTE   *Although you can use an existing Project file as the consolidated Project file, it doesn't usually make sense to do so because you will no longer be able to work with the existing project independent from the other subprojects included in the consolidated file.*

2. Display the file in Gantt Chart view.

To do so, click the Gantt Chart icon on the View Bar.

3. Select the Task Name box for the row where you want to insert the subproject.

If your consolidated Project file contains tasks, select the task above which you want the subproject inserted.

4. Choose the Insert menu's Project command.

Project displays the Insert Project dialog box, as shown in Figure C-1.

Figure C-1   The Insert Project dialog box.

5. Open the folder storing the file.

Use the icons along the left side of the Insert Project dialog box and the list box of folders and files to locate the file. When you find it, select it by clicking it.

- To insert a file you've recently accessed, click the History icon to browse shortcuts to recently accessed files.

- If you have Microsoft Windows 95 or 98, click the My Documents icon to insert a file from the default storage location for Microsoft Office documents. If you have Windows NT, click the Personal icon.

- To insert a file from the Windows desktop, click the Desktop icon.

- To insert a file stored in a location other than one designated by an icon (such as a network drive), use the Look In drop-down list box and the large list box below to select the drive and folder location.

6. **Specify whether you want to link or embed the subproject.**

   Select the Link To Project check box if you want changes in the consolidated project file updated in the subproject file and vice versa. Clear the Link To Project check box if you want to simply paste the subproject into the consolidated Project file.

7. **Click the Insert button.**

   Project inserts the subproject in the row above the selected row, as shown in Figure C-2. The Information column displays an icon reminding you that the subproject is inserted from another file. If you rest your mouse pointer over the icon, Project displays a ScreenTip that describes the link.

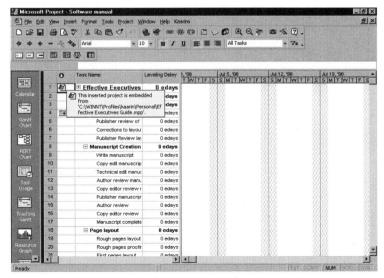

Figure C-2   Creating a consolidated Project file.

8. **Repeat actions 3 through 7 for other projects you want to insert in the consolidated project.**

9. **If you want to work with the consolidated project again, save it after you're finished inserting projects.**

You can work with the tasks in a consolidated Project file the same way you work with tasks in all other Project files. For example, you link tasks (regardless of the subproject to which they belong) as described in Step 3. If you make changes to the consolidated project and if you chose to link to the source projects when you initially created the consolidated project, Project asks you whether you want to save changes to each of the source projects.

TIP   *To focus on certain subprojects, you can hide others. Just click the minus sign beside the subproject's summary task.*

Updating Links of Source Projects

If you chose to link the source projects to the consolidated project, you will need to update the links if you move the source file. To do so, take the following actions:

1. **Open the consolidated Project file.**

If necessary, click the Gantt Chart icon on the View Bar to display the file in Gantt Chart view.

2. **Select the project you need to relink.**

To do so, click the inserted project's name in the Task Name column.

3. **Click the Task Information toolbar button.**

Project displays the Inserted Project Information dialog box.

4. **Click the Advanced tab.**

Figure C-3 shows the Advanced tab of the Inserted Project Information dialog box.

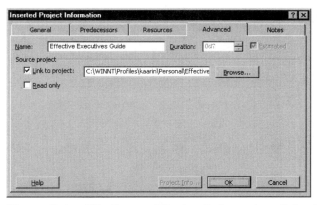

Figure C-3   The Inserted Project Information dialog box.

5. Specify the new path to the source file.

Enter a new location in the Link To Project text box, or click the Browse button to locate the source file.

TIP   *To unlink the source file, clear the Link To Project check box.*

6. Click OK.

Linking Tasks Across Separate Project Files

If you don't want to create a consolidated project, you can still link tasks across projects. To do so, you need to create external links. To work with external links, take the following actions:

1. Open the project containing the task you want to link to another file.

If necessary, display the project in Gantt Chart view.

2. Click in the Predecessors column for the task you want to link.

3. Enter the path to the project, a backslash, and the task ID number within that project.

For example, if the task to which you want to link is number 6 in a project named September in your My Documents folder, you would enter the following:

C:\MY DOCUMENTS\SEPTEMBER.MPP\6

Figure C-4 shows an example of an external link in a project.

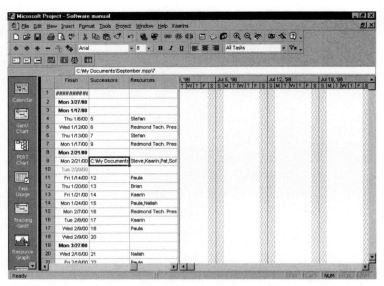

Figure C-4   Linking a task to a task in an external project.

NOTE   *You edit external links the same way you edit internal links. "Step 3: Schedule Project Tasks" describes editing links.*

CUSTOMIZE PROJECT

In This Appendix

- Customizing toolbars
- Customizing menus
- Customizing a table
- Customizing the Gantt chart
- Changing the default view

As you work with Microsoft Project 2000 and become more familiar with it, you'll probably eventually wish that you could change certain features. You might, for example, prefer that your project always opens in a view other than the Gantt Chart view, or you might want to replace the Task Notes button with another button that you'd actually use. The good new is that you can change most of the elements in Project, and in this appendix we walk you through the steps.

Customizing Toolbars

By default, Project displays the Standard and Formatting toolbars. To hide either of these or display other toolbars, you choose the View menu's Toolbars command and then click the name of a toolbar on the submenu to hide or display it. In addition, you can add and remove buttons from the default toolbar, and you can even create completely new toolbars.

Adding and Deleting Buttons

You can add and delete toolbar buttons from the default toolbars in a couple of ways. Let's look at the simplest and quickest way first. At the far right on each of the default toolbars, you'll see a little down arrow. When you place your cursor over this arrow, you'll see a ScreenTip that tells you this is the More Buttons button. When you click the More Buttons button, you'll see the Add Or Remove Buttons button. Clicking this button displays a drop-down list of the available buttons for that toolbar. Figure D-1 shows the available buttons for the Standard toolbar. A check mark preceding a button name indicates that the button is currently displayed. To remove the button, simply click its name. To restore a button, click its name again.

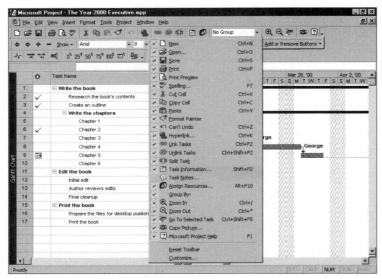

Figure D-1 The buttons on the Standard toolbar.

But what if you want to, for example, display a Tracking toolbar button on the Standard toolbar? To add a button to a toolbar, take the following actions:

1. **Choose the Tools menu's Customize command, and then choose the submenu's Toolbars command.**

   Project displays the Customize dialog box, as shown in Figure D-2.

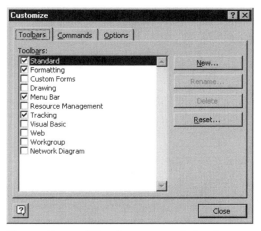

Figure D-2   The Customize dialog box.

2. If necessary, click the Toolbars tab.

3. Make sure that the toolbar that contains the button you want to add is displayed.

Make sure the check box is selected.

4. Click the Commands tab.

Project displays the Commands tab of the Customize dialog box, as shown in Figure D-3.

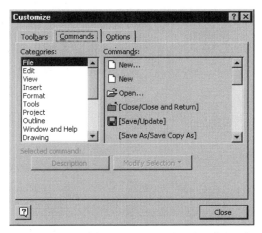

Figure D-3   The Commands tab of the Customize dialog box.

5. **Select the category that contains the command you want to add.**

   In the Categories list, select the toolbar button you want to add.

6. **Click the command, and then drag it to the toolbar on which you want to display it.**

   Project adds the button to the toolbar.

7. **Click Close in the Customize dialog box.**

   To delete a button from a toolbar, open the Customize dialog box and then click and drag the button off the toolbar.

TIP   *To restore a toolbar to its original settings, open the Customize dialog box, select the name of the toolbar, and click the Reset button.*

Changing Button Images

If you were designing the Project interface, would you have chosen some different little pictures for some of the buttons? Well, to a certain extent, you can play designer. You can change a button's image to one of the other predefined images that are included with Project, and you can edit those images.

Selecting a New Image

To select a new image for an existing toolbar button, take the following actions:

1. **Display the toolbar that contains the button whose image you want to change.**

   To display a toolbar, choose the View menu's Toolbars command and then choose the toolbar from the submenu.

2. **Choose the Tools menu's Customize command, and then choose the submenu's Toolbars command.**

   Project displays the Customize dialog box.

3. **Click the Commands tab.**

4. **Click the button for which you want to select a new image.**

5. **Click the Modify Selection button, and then choose Change Button Image.**

   Project displays a palette of button images, as shown in Figure D-4.

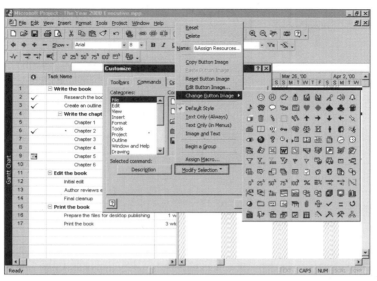

Figure D-4   Click an image to display it on a button instead of the current image.

6. Click Close in the Customize dialog box.

To restore a button's original image, take actions 1 through 3, click the Modify Selection button, choose Reset Button Image, and then click Close in the Customize dialog box.

Editing an Image

If you want to edit a current image instead of selecting a new image, take the following actions:

1. Display the toolbar that contains the button whose image you want to edit.

To display a toolbar, choose the View menu's Toolbars command and then choose the toolbar from the submenu.

2. Choose the Tools menu's Customize command, and then choose the submenu's Toolbars command.

Project displays the Customize dialog box.

3. Click the Commands tab.

4. Click the button for which you want to select a new image.

5. Click the Modify Selection button, and then choose Edit Button Image.

Project displays the Button Editor dialog box, as shown in Figure D-5.

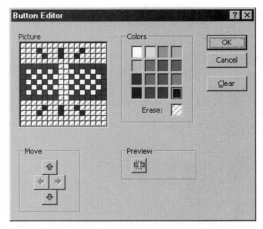

Figure D-5   The Button Editor dialog box.

6. **To change the colors of an image, click a color and then click a pixel in the picture.**

NOTE   *An image is composed of many tiny squares, as you can see in Figure D-5. Each square is called a* pixel *(short for* picture element*).*

7. **To remove color from a pixel, click the Erase square and then click the pixel.**

8. **If you can't see all of a large button in the Picture box, click an arrow in the Move box.**

9. **When you've finished redesigning the button, click OK.**

Click Close when you're finished to close the Customize dialog box.

Creating a New Toolbar

If you're working on a project that involves using a number of buttons often and these buttons are on various toolbars, you might want to consider creating a new toolbar that includes only these buttons. To do so, take the following actions:

1. **Choose the Tools menu's Customize command, and then choose the submenu's Toolbars command.**

Project displays the Customize dialog box.

2. **Click New.**

Project displays the New Toolbar dialog box, as shown in Figure D-6.

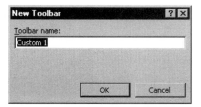

Figure D-6   The New Toolbar dialog box.

3. **Enter a name for your toolbar in the Toolbar Name box (perhaps the name of your project), and click OK.**

A small toolbar will appear on your screen, as shown in Figure D-7. You can move this toolbar to any location on the screen that you like. Simply click the title bar and then drag the toolbar. In addition, you'll see that the name of your new toolbar has been added to the Toolbars list in the Toolbars tab.

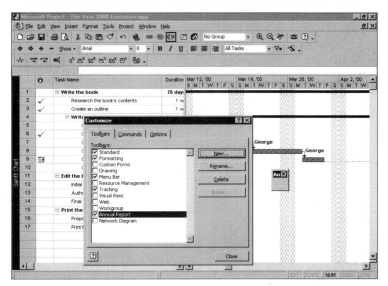

Figure D-7   You can drag tools to populate the toolbar you just created.

NOTE   *You may need to move the Customize dialog box in order to see your new toolbar.*

4. **Click the Commands tab.**

5. **Select a category, and then click a command and drag it to your new toolbar.**

6. **Optionally, insert divider lines between buttons.**

Select the button to the right of where you want the line, click the Modify Selection button, and then choose Begin A Group.

7. **Click Close in the Customize dialog box.**

To remove a toolbar you've created, select its name in the Toolbars list on the Toolbars tab of the Customize dialog box, and click the Delete button. When Project asks if you're sure you want to delete this toolbar, click OK.

Customizing Menus

You customize menus in the same way that you customize toolbars, that is, by using the Customize dialog box. But before we get into the specifics, we need to take a look at personalized menus. In the Microsoft Office 2000 suite of products, of which Project is a part, the default setting is for menus to display the commands you most often use first and then display the full menu after a short delay. This feature pleases some users and annoys others. If you are among the latter, you can change this feature. To do so, take the following actions:

1. **Choose the Tools menu's Customize command, and then choose the submenu's Toolbars command.**

Project displays the Customize dialog box.

2. **Click the Options tab.**

Project displays the Options tab of the Customize dialog box, as shown in Figure D-8.

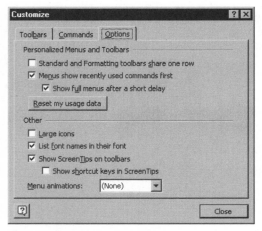

Figure D-8   The Options tab of the Customize dialog box.

3. Clear the Menus Show Recently Used Commands First check box, and clear the Show Full Menus After A Short Delay check box.

If you want to conserve screen real estate, select the Standard And Formatting Toolbars Share One Row check box. When you do so, Project combines these two toolbars. Obviously, there isn't enough room for all the buttons. To display those that are omitted, click the More Buttons button at the far right of the toolbar.

4. Click Close.

To return your display to its original setting, click the Reset My Usage Data button on the Options tab of the Customize dialog box. Use the options in the Other section of this tab to display large icons, display font names in their font, and show or hide ScreenTips and their associated shortcut keys. If you want to animate menus, select an option from the Menu Animations drop-down list box.

Adding New Commands

As previously mentioned, you add commands to menus in much the same way that you add buttons to toolbars. To add a command to an existing menu, take the following actions:

1. Choose the Tools menu's Customize command, and then choose the submenu's Toolbars command.

Project displays the Customize dialog box.

2. Click the Commands tab.

3. Select a category, and then click the title of the menu to which you want to add a command.

Project opens the list of commands.

4. Click a command in the Commands list, and drag it to the location on the menu where you want it.

5. Click Close in the Customize dialog box.

Adding New Menus

Adding a new menu is similar to adding a new toolbar. To add a new menu, take the following actions:

1. Make sure that the menu bar is displayed on your screen.

2. Choose the Tools menu's Customize command, and then choose the submenu's Toolbars command.

Project displays the Customize dialog box.

3. Click the Commands tab.

4. Scroll to the bottom of the Categories list, and select New Menu.

   New Menu now appears in the Commands list, as shown in Figure D-9.

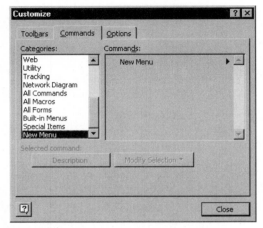

Figure D-9   The New Menu command now appears in the Commands list.

5. Click New Menu in the Commands list, and drag it up to the menu bar.

6. Click the Modify Selection button, and type a name for your new menu in the Name box.

   When you click the Modify Selection button, Project opens a menu of commands. Click outside the Modify Selection menu to close it.

7. Select a category, and then click a command and drag it to the menu.

   Drop it in the empty box that appears beneath your new menu.

8. Click Close in the Customize dialog box.

To remove a new menu you've added, open the Customize dialog box, click the new menu, drag it off the menu bar, and then click Close in the Customize dialog box.

Customizing a Table

You can also customize existing tables by inserting rows, deleting rows, changing the date format or the row height, and so on. And you can create new tables. We'll look first at how to make some changes to existing tables.

WARNING *There is no Reset button in the More Tables dialog box, so make a copy of a table before editing it because your changes are permanent after you save the file. To make a copy of a table, in the More Tables dialog box, select the table name and then click the Copy button.*

Changing an Existing Table

You learned in Step 3 how to insert rows in a table, but you can also insert columns. Depending on the nature of your project, you may find that you need to track information that doesn't logically fit in any of the predefined columns. To add a column to the Entry table, take the following actions:

1. **Open your project in Gantt Chart view.**

2. **Choose the View menu's Table command, and choose the submenu's More Tables command.**

   Project displays the More Tables dialog box, as shown in Figure D-10.

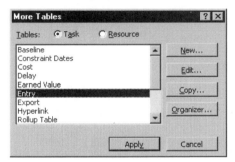

Figure D-10 The More Tables dialog box.

3. **Select the name of the table you want to edit, and click the Copy button.**

   Project displays the Table Definition dialog box for that project. Figure D-11 shows the Table Definition dialog box for the book-publishing project.

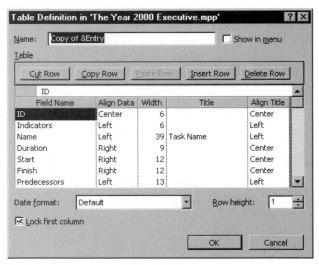

Figure D-11 The Table Definition dialog box.

4. Now you can do any of the following:

- Display the table's name in the More Tables dialog box by typing a new name in the Name box and selecting the Show In Menu check box.

- Delete a row by selecting a field in the Field Name column, and clicking the Delete Row button.

- Insert a row above the selected row by selecting a field, and clicking the Insert Row button.

- Change a column name by selecting it from the Field Name column and then selecting a new field name from the drop-down list.

- Change how the data are aligned in a column by selecting the column in the Align Data column and selecting Center, Right, or Left from the drop-down list.

- Change the width of a column by selecting it in the Width column and selecting a character width from the drop-down list.

- Change a title by selecting the column name in the Title column and typing a new name.

- Change how the title aligns by selecting it in the Align Title column and selecting Center, Right, or Left from the drop-down list.

- Change the date format by selecting an entry from the Date Format drop-down list box.

- Change the row height by using the Row Height spin box.

5. When you're finished making changes, click OK.

To insert a new column in a table, take the following actions:

1. Right-click the column head to the right of where you want to insert a new column.

2. Choose the shortcut menu's Insert Column command.

Project displays the Column Definition dialog box, as shown in Figure D-12.

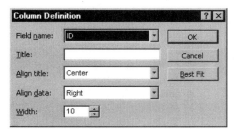

Figure D-12 The Column Definition dialog box.

3. Select a field type for the column.

Select an entry from the Field Name drop-down list box.

4. Name the column.

Enter a name in the Title box.

5. Specify how you want the title to align.

Select Center, Right, or Left from the Align Title drop-down list box.

6. Specify how you want the data to align in the cells.

Select Center, Right, or Left from the Align Data drop-down list box.

7. Rather than specify the character width, click the Best Fit button.

8. Click OK.

Figure D-13 shows a new column, Department, inserted in the book-publishing project.

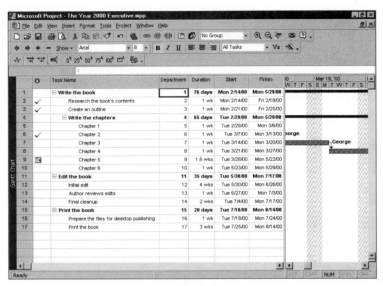

Figure D-13 A new column, Department, has been inserted between the Task Name column and the Duration column.

Creating a New Table

To create an entirely new table, take the following actions:

1. Choose the View menu's Table command, and then choose the submenu's More Tables command.

Project displays the More Tables dialog box, as shown in Figure D-14.

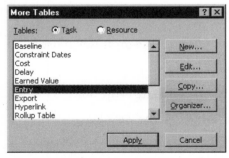

Figure D-14 The More Tables dialog box.

2. Click the New button.

Project displays the Table Definition dialog box, as shown in Figure D-15.

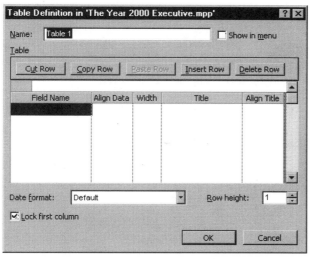

Figure D-15 The Table Definition dialog box.

3. Name the table.

Enter a name in the Name box.

4. Specify a field name.

Click in the Field Name column, and select a field name from the drop-down list.

5. Specify the data alignment.

Click in the Align Data column, and select an alignment from the drop-down list.

6. Click in the Width column, and accept the default character width.

You can adjust this width later by simply clicking between column titles.

7. Click in the Title column, and enter a name for the column.

8. Specify the title alignment.

Click in the Align Title column, and select an alignment from the drop-down list.

9. Repeat actions 4 through 9 to add more fields to your table.

TIP   *Use the Cut Row, Copy Row, Paste Row, Insert Row, and Delete Row buttons to facilitate field entry.*

10. Specify the date format.

Accept the default date format, or select another from the Date Format drop-down list.

11. **Adjust the height of all rows.**

    Use the Row Height spin box to do this.

12. **If you want the first column of your table to remain on the screen when you scroll across, leave the Lock First Column check box selected.**

13. **When you're finished, click OK.**

    Back in the More Tables dialog box, click the Apply button to display your table on the screen.

Customizing the Gantt Chart

As you know from the steps in the first part of this book, you can change how the timescale is displayed in the Gantt chart by clicking on the Zoom In and Zoom Out buttons on the Standard toolbar, but you can also change the display of the Gantt chart in other ways. You can change the display of nonworking time, change the appearance of the bars, and add gridlines to a chart. We'll start with how to change the display of nonworking time.

Changing the Display of Nonworking Time

By default, the vertical bar that represents nonworking time is shown behind the task bars and thus the task bar appears to be running through nonworking days. If you find this confusing, you can change the display for nonworking time. Here are some other options:

• Display the nonworking time vertical bar in front of the task bar.

• Hide the nonworking time vertical bar.

• Display the nonworking time vertical bar in a different color and with a different pattern.

To change how Project displays nonworking time, take the following actions:

1. **In Gantt Chart view, double-click the vertical gray bar that represents nonworking time.**

   Project displays the Nonworking Time tab of the Timescale dialog box, as shown in Figure D-16.

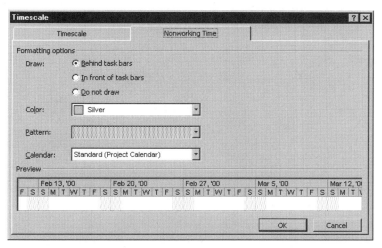

Figure D-16 The Nonworking Time tab of the Timescale dialog box.

2. Click the In Front Of Task Bars option button.

Project displays the nonworking time bar in front of the task bars, as shown in Figure D-17.

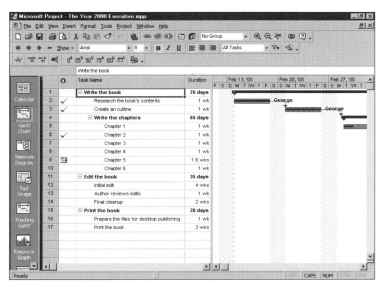

Figure D-17 Nonworking time displayed in front of the task bars.

3. If you would rather not display nonworking time, click the Do Not Draw option button.

Figure D-18 shows how this looks.

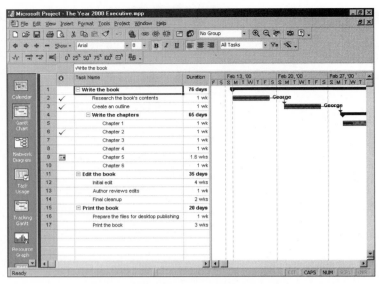

Figure D-18 Nonworking time is not displayed in this chart.

You can also choose to display the nonworking time bar in another color by selecting a color from the Color drop-down list. Change the pattern using the Pattern drop-down list.

4. When you're finished, click OK.

Changing the Appearance of Bars

To change the appearance of a single bar in the Gantt chart, take the following actions:

1. Double-click the bar.

Project displays the Format Bar dialog box, as shown in Figure D-19.

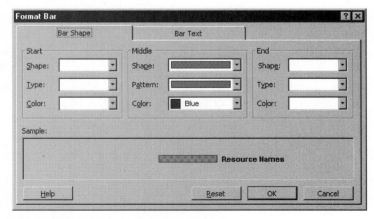

Figure D-19 The Format Bar dialog box.

2. **Change the shape, pattern, type, and color of the bar.**

   To do this, use the options on the Bar Shape tab, as shown in Figure D-19.

3. **Click the Bar Text tab to change the position of text and to change the displayed text.**

   Figure D-20 shows this tab.

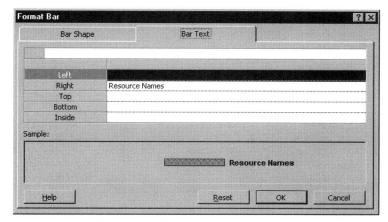

Figure D-20 The Bar Text tab of the Format Bar dialog box.

4. **When you're finished, click OK.**

   To return the bar to its original style, click the Reset button in the Format Bar dialog box.

Changing the Appearance of All Bars

To change the appearance of all bars in the Gantt chart, take the following actions:

1. **Double-click anywhere in the working area of the chart.**

   Project displays the Bar Styles dialog box, as shown in Figure D-21.

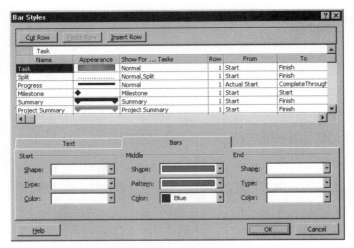

Figure D-21 The Bar Styles dialog box.

2. **Select an item in the Appearance column, and then make your changes in the bottom portion of the dialog box.**

   This area is similar to the Bar Shape tab of the Format Bar dialog box.

3. **When you're finished, click OK.**

Adding Gridlines to the Chart

Some users find it helpful to extend the lines that separate items in the Entry table all the way through the Gantt chart. To add these gridlines to your chart, take the following actions:

1. **Right-click anywhere in the Gantt chart, and choose the shortcut menu's Gridlines command.**

   Project displays the Gridlines dialog box, as shown in Figure D-22.

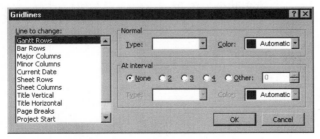

Figure D-22 The Gridlines dialog box.

2. Select Gantt Rows in the Line To Change list.

3. Select a line type in the Type drop-down list, and select a color for your gridlines in the Color drop-down list.

If you want to spread your guidelines, select an interval. None displays gridlines spaced an item's width apart, 2 displays gridlines two item's widths apart, and so on.

4. When you're finished, click OK.

Figure D-23 shows gridlines added to the chart in the book-publishing project.

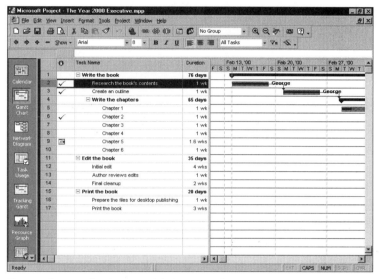

Figure D-23 Gridlines added to the Gantt chart.

Changing the Default View

If you typically work in a view other than Gantt Chart view, you might want to make it easy on yourself and change the default view. To do so, take the following actions:

1. Choose the Tools menu's Options command.

Project displays the Options dialog box.

2. Select a view from the Default View drop-down list.

This is the view you will see every time you open a project.

3. Click OK.

GLOSSARY

Accrual method

The practice of recording costs for **resources** when the costs are incurred, which may be at the start of the **task**, at the finish of the task, or prorated.

ACWP

An abbreviation for Actual Cost of Work Performed. The actual cost of work already completed by a specific date.

AutoFilter

A **filter** that applies to a single column in a **Gantt chart**.

BAC

An abbreviation for Budgeted At Completion. This amount shows the total planned cost.

Baseline

A snapshot of a **project** that shows all aspects of a project. You can use it to compare actual progress with planned progress.

BCWP

An abbreviation for Budgeted Cost of Work Performed. This amount shows the planned value of the work completed.

BCWS

An abbreviation for Budgeted Cost of Work Scheduled. This amount shows the planned value of the work originally scheduled.

Chart

A graphical representation of **project** information.

Combination view

A split window that shows one **view** in the top pane and another view in the bottom pane.

Constraint

A restriction that limits the start or finish of a **task.**

Critical path

The series of **tasks** that must be completed on time in order for a **project** to finish on **schedule.**

Critical task

A task on the **critical path.**

CV

An abbreviation for Cost Variance. This amount shows the difference between **BCWP** and **ACWP.**

Deliverable

The outcome that must be produced to complete a **project** or a **task.**

Dependency

A relationship between **tasks.** Because one task depends on another, it might need to start before or after the other task or at some point during work on the other task.

Duration

The time it will take to complete a **task**. If a task will take one week to complete, for example, you can say its duration equals one week.

EAC

An abbreviation for Estimated At Completion. This amount shows the total actual cost incurred to date plus the remaining planned costs.

Earned value

The value of work completed; the same as **BCWP**.

Export Map

Instructions about what and in what format Microsoft Project information will be exported to another application.

Filter

A Microsoft Project tool that you can use to display only certain information about a **project**, for example, only **tasks** that have been completed by a specified date.

Fixed cost

A cost that does not increase or decrease over time, for example, a one-time licensing fee.

Gantt chart

A graphical representation of information in a **project**; named for Henry Gantt who in the nineteenth century introduced this method of displaying information in a bar chart/spreadsheet fashion.

GIF

An abbreviation for Graphics Interchange Format. A file format originally developed for on-screen display that results in relatively small graphics files.

Highlighted Filter view

Displays **filtered** tasks or **resources** in a color different from that of the other **tasks** or resources.

HTML

An abbreviation for HyperText Markup Language; the language used to create documents that display in a web browser.

Hyperlink

Text or a graphic in an **HTML** document that displays in a distinct manner (usually in a different color and underlined). Clicking a hyperlink takes you to another resource that can be on your computer, your **local area network** or **intranet,** or the **Internet.**

Internet

The world's largest computer network, connecting tens of millions of users.

Intranet

A private corporate network that uses the **Internet** technology.

Isolated Filter view

Displays only the **filtered** tasks or **resources**.

Lag time

The amount of down time between the end of one **task** and the start of another.

Lead time

The amount of time that dependent **tasks** overlap. For example, if one task can start when the other is half finished, the lead time is 50 percent.

Legend

The information at the bottom of a printed **chart** that explains the graphical elements used in the chart, such as lines and symbols.

Leveling

Resolving **resource** conflicts. You can level resources manually, or you can let Microsoft Project do it automatically.

Linking

Creating a **dependency** between **tasks**.

Local area network

Abbreviated LAN. A group of computers and peripherals that are connected and that can share resources. A LAN usually connects computers within a single building.

Milestone

A **task** that indicates the beginning or end of a task and that is a significant event in a **project**.

MPD

The file extension that saves an entire **project** file in database format.

MPP

The default project file extension.

MPT

The Microsoft Project template file extension.

MPX

The file extension that saves a **project** file in ASCII, record-based text format so that it can be transferred between applications that support the MPX file format.

Nonworking time

Weekends, holidays, or any other dates on which the people involved in a **project** do not work on the project.

Outdent

Move a **task** to the left (and thus to a higher level) in the Task Name field so that it becomes a **summary task.**

Overallocation

Assigning more **tasks** to a **resource** than the resource can accomplish in the time allotted.

PERT

A method for tracking **task** flow. PERT is an acronym for Program Evaluation and Review Technique and was developed in the 1950s by the Special Projects Office of the U.S. Navy.

PivotTable

A Microsoft Excel table that summarizes information into rows and columns that you can rotate.

Predecessor

A **task** that must be accomplished before some other task, known as a **successor,** can be started.

Project

A set of **tasks** that collectively achieve some objective. Typically, the tasks must be accomplished in a specified order and require **resources.**

Project management

The art and science of organizing **tasks** in such a way as to control their progress.

Report

A method for organizing and formatting **project** information so that it can be printed.

Resource pool

A group of **resources** that you can use to make **task** assignments.

Resources

The workers and tools needed to accomplish a **task.**

Schedule

The time and sequence of **tasks** in a **project.**

Slack

The amount of time that a **task** can slip before it affects a **dependency** or the **project** completion date.

Slippage

The delay of a **task** from its **baseline** plan.

Sorting

Rearranging information in a **project** so that it is displayed in a different way. For example, you might sort **resources** in alphabetic order.

Stakeholder

Any person who is involved or affected by a **project.**

Subtask

A **task** that is subordinate to a **summary task.**

Successor

A **task** that can be accomplished only after a **predecessor,** or prerequisite task, has been completed.

Summary task

A **task** that is made up of subordinate tasks.

SV

An abbreviation for Schedule Variance. This amount shows the difference between the **BCWS** and the **BCWP.**

Task

The basic building block of a **project,** a task constitutes a discrete amount of work often performed by a specific person at a specific time.

Task ID

A number that Microsoft Project associates with each **task.**

Template

A predefined pattern that you can use as the basis for setting up a **project.** To work with a template, choose the File menu's New command, and select a template from the lists on the Project Templates tab or the Office 97 Templates tab.

Timescale

A graphical representation that appears at the top of a **chart** and shows a calendar in various **views** that you can define. By default, the timescale shows the weeks and days.

VAC

An abbreviation for Variance At Completion. This amount shows the difference between the **BAC** and the **EAC.**

View

One of the various ways to display information in Microsoft Project.

WBS

An abbreviation for Work Breakdown Structure. This **project-management** system organizes **tasks** to facilitate detailed **reporting** and tracking of costs. Microsoft Project uses the WBS outlining structure.

Work

The total number of hours required to complete a **task.**

Workgroup

A group of people who work on the same **project.**

Index

flowcharts. *See* Network Diagram view

fonts, formatting, 46

footers, 139

Format Bar dialog box, 252–53, 254

formatting

    Gantt chart bars, 252–54

    task notes, 46

Formatting toolbar, 89

G

Gantt charts, defined, 17–18, 259

Gantt Chart view

    adding gridlines, 254–55

    adding progress lines, 185–86

    vs. Calendar view, 19–20

    changing bar appearance, 252–54

    changing default view, 255

    changing display of nonworking time, 250–52

    changing timescale, 97–98

    copying information to Word, 163

    customizing charts, 250–55

    exporting information to Excel, 156

    illustrated, 18, 20

    inserting subprojects into, 230–32

    overview, 17–18, 114

    personal charts, 208–9

    in Print Preview, 133

    showing completed tasks, 171

    with summary bar, 91

    and Task Details Form view, 172–73

    and Task Form view, 172

    and Update Tasks dialog box, 173–74

    using to manage resources, 20–22

GIF files, 164–65, 259

graphics files, copying Project information to, 164–65

graphs. *See* charts

gridlines, adding to Gantt charts, 254–55

H

headers and footers, 137–39

Help window, 26

hiding toolbars, 235

Highlighted Filter view, defined, 260

HTML, 158–59, 260

human resources. *See* people resources

hyperlinks, defined, 260. *See also* linking;
  Microsoft Project Central

I

Incomplete Tasks filter, 100, 104

Inserted Project Information dialog box, 232–33

Insert Project dialog box, 230–31

interactive filters, 108

Internet, defined, 260

intranets, defined, 260

Isolated Filter view, defined, 260

K

keyboard shortcuts, for macros, 226, 227

L

lag time. *See also* slack

    adding between tasks, 50

    defined, 260

    minimizing, 219–21

late finish dates, 8, 10–11

late start dates, 8, 11–12

Layout dialog box, 217

lead time, defined, 260

left-aligning text, 46

legends, chart, 140–41, 260

Leveling Gantt view, 114, 123–24

leveling resources, 76–80, 261

linking. *See also* dependencies, task; hyperlinks

    defined, 3, 261

    tasks across project files, 233–34

    tasks by dependencies, 3, 4, 48–49

    tasks in subproject files to consolidated project
      file, 231, 232

local area networks, defined, 261

M

macros
  assigning keyboard shortcuts to, 226, 227
  for automating repetitive tasks, 225–27
  describing in Record Macro dialog box, 226
  naming, 226
  recording, 225–27
  running, 227
  storing, 226
margins, page, 136
materials, as resources, 59–61
menus
  adding, 243–44
  adding new commands, 243
  customizing, 242–44
  personalized, 242–43
messages, e-mail
  creating rules, 206–7
  overview, 191–92
  reading in Inbox, 205–6
  sending project files as attachments, 192–93
  TeamAssign messages, 195–98
  TeamStatus messages, 199
  TeamUpdate messages, 198
  using to assign projects, 195–98
Microsoft Access, exporting Project files to, 157–58
Microsoft Excel, exporting Project files to, 154–56
Microsoft Project
  Calendar view, 19–20, 114, 117–18
  customizing, 235–55
  Gantt Chart view, 17–18
  vs. Project 98, 28
  role in project management, 17
  setting up Browser Module, 200–202
  starting, 26
  using to manage resources, 20–22
  using to monitor project time, resources, and costs, 22–23

Microsoft Project Central
  See also Browser Module
  adding new tasks, 209
  installing, 199–200
  navigating, 205
  requesting status reports, 209–10
  web site, 203, 204–5
Microsoft Project window, 41, 42, 43, 52
Microsoft Word, copying Project information to, 162–63
Milestone Date Rollup view, 114
Milestone Rollup view, 114
milestones, 5, 52, 261
Milestones filter, 100, 104
MMP files, defined, 261
More Filters dialog box, 105–6
More Tables dialog box, 116, 245, 248
More Views dialog box, 111, 114, 122
most-likely scenarios, 214, 215
moving tasks, 94–95
MPD files, defined, 261
MPT files, defined, 261
MPX files, defined, 261
multiple projects, 229–34

N

naming
  calendars, 33, 69
  people resources, 58
  project files, 27
  tables, 249
Network Diagram view
  changing, 216–17
  illustrated, 18, 215
  overview, 18–19, 114, 119–20
  vs. PERT analysis, 215
  toolbar, 217
  using, 215–17
networks. See workgroups
New Toolbar dialog box, 240–41

W

WBS (Work Breakdown Structure)
  customized codes, 224
  defined, 264
  displaying codes, 223–24
  example of numbering, 222–23
  inserting column for codes, 224
  vs. outline codes, 225
web pages, saving project files as, 158–59
web server, setting up with Microsoft Project
  Central, 199–200
what-if analysis. *See* PERT analysis
Word. *See* Microsoft Word
work, defined, 264
workdays, typical, exceptions, 72
Workgroup Mail dialog box, 196
workgroups. *See also* Microsoft Project Central
  assigning tasks or projects via e-mail, 195–98
  communicating about project files, 193–99
  defined, 264
  Project 2000 features for, 199–211
  setting up in Project 2000, 202–3
Workload reports category, 145
Work table, 183–85
  for resources, 184–85
  for tasks, 183–84
workweek, typical, exceptions, 72

The manuscript for this book was prepared and submitted to Redmond Technology Press in electronic form. Text files were prepared using Microsoft Word 2000. Pages were composed using PageMaker 6.5 for Windows, with text in Frutiger and Caslon. Composed files were delivered to the printer as electronic prepress files.

Interior Design

Stefan Knorr

Project Editor

Paula Thurman

Technical Editor

Brian Milbrath

Indexer

Julie Kawabata

ONE SIMPLE QUESTION.

DO YOU USE EXCEL FOR BUSINESS?

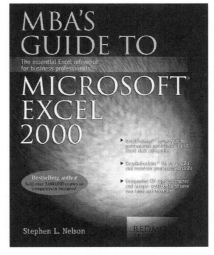

MBA's Guide to Microsoft Excel 2000: The essential Excel reference for business professionals is the only book that specifically describes how you can more easily, more productively and more powerfully use Microsoft® Excel 2000 in business.

QuickPrimers™ move you to professional proficiency in all Excel skill categories.
The *MBA's Guide to Microsoft Excel 2000* begins at the beginning. If you need it, you first get friendly help on all the basics, including building simple worksheets and creating charts you can use for both analysis and presentation. If you don't need this help, you can easily skip it.

Step-by-step approach makes even Excel's most powerful tools easy to use.
Once you've become comfortable with Excel, *MBA's Guide to Microsoft Excel 2000* moves you beyond the basics. You get easy-to-understand, jargon-free help on using all of Excel's business tools including PivotTables, PivotCharts, Solver, BackSolver, and Small Business Manager.

EasyRefreshers™ let you build and maintain your business skills. As you advance, *MBA's Guide to Microsoft Excel 2000* moves on and describes how to use Excel's often poorly documented tools for statistical analysis, financial calculations, sharing corporate data, and optimization modeling. Discussions usually start with *EasyRefreshers™* that let you update old skills or acquire new core business skills.

Works for all business users. Written for anyone who wants to use Excel as a business tool for powering better business decisions, *MBA's Guide to Microsoft Excel 2000* works for MBA students, MBA graduates, Excel users with undergraduate degrees in business or a related field—and for anyone else who's serious about using Excel as a tool for making better business decisions.

Companion CD supplies starter and sample workbooks. The *MBA's Guide to Microsoft Excel 2000* companion CD supplies starter Excel workbooks for business planning, profit-volume-cost analysis, break-even calculations, capital investment budgeting, asset depreciation and debt amortization so you get a head start on creating your own workbooks. The CD also supplies samples of all the workbooks discussed in the book.

Available at bookstores everywhere and at all online bookstores.

ISBN 0-9672981-0-5

U.S. $39.95 Business Applications / Microsoft Excel